The Spokesman
Legacies of Harm
Edited by Ken Coates
Published by Spokesman for the
Bertrand Russell Peace Foundation

Spokesman 96   2007

CONTENTS

Editorial	3	*Ken Coates*
45 minute threat	8	*John Major interviewed by Elinor Goodman*
Stones	9	*John Berger*
Eyeless in Gaza	19	*Usamah Hamden* *Michael Ancram MP* *Jonathan Lehrle, Mark Perry*
Israel	31	*Gabriel Kolko*
The man without a country	35	*James Alexander Thom*
Kurt is up in Heaven now	38	*Kurt Vonnegut*
Two Poems	46	*Alexis Lykiard*
Star Wars Again	47	*Noam Chomsky*
Manipulating the Security Council	49	*Hans von Sponeck interviewed by Silvia Cattori*
Polonium-210 in London	59	*Zhores Medvedev*
Dossier	71	*Alvaro de Soto* *Jimmy Carter* *Johan Galtung*
Reviews	81	*Michael Barratt Brown* *J.E.Mortimer* *Ken Coates* *Stan Newens* *Tony Simpson* *Henry McCubbin*

Cover: With thanks to Steve Bell.
Printed by the Russell Press Ltd., Nottingham, UK

ISSN 1367-7748   ISBN 0 85124 747 4

Subscriptions
Institutions £35.00
Individuals £20.00 (UK)
£25.00 (ex UK)

Back issues available on request

A CIP catalogue record for this book is available from the British Library

Published by the
Bertrand Russell Peace Foundation Ltd.,
Russell House
Bulwell Lane
Nottingham NG6 0BT
England
Tel. 0115 9784504
email:
elfeuro@compuserve.com
www.spokesmanbooks.com
www.russfound.org

Editorial Board:
Michael Barratt Brown
Ken Coates
John Daniels
Ken Fleet
Stuart Holland
Tony Simpson

www.unitetheunion.org.uk
www.tgwu.org.uk

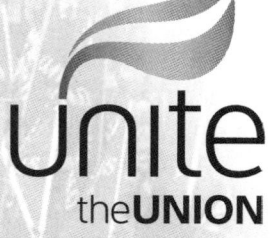

Fighting for peace and justice

DEREK SIMPSON AND **TONY WOODLEY**
Joint General Secretaries

T&G section

Editorial
Legacies of Harm

The British press has already celebrated the departure of Tony Blair from Number Ten Downing Street with appropriate pomp. A high sense of relief throughout the country meant that his resignation was received, by and large, rather charitably. There will be plenty of time to recall his incompetence, his authoritarianism, the manifold abuses of his conduct of office.

There are innumerable British people who have reason to remember their former Prime Minister with rancour. On the other hand, Casino operators and other bandits will mourn his loss. There are a number of beneficiaries of his rule who will, for a little while, celebrate his kindness, his winning smile, his decency. But these pleasant qualities have not been widely noticed in Iraq. There, the dead speak more loudly than the beneficiaries. One small thing of note is the report that Gordon Brown, newly installed in the premiership, was reported to have telephoned the family of a young man, who had just been killed, to commiserate. If this is true, it is something which Mr. Blair apparently never found it in himself to do.

We do not yet know how far the British Government will change its policies towards Iraq. The newspapers speculate on slight evidence, grasping at straws. Some straws may be rather thin, such as the rumour that the new Foreign Secretary has doubts about the war. He has apparently also had doubts about expressing those doubts, so we have to wait for more tangible evidence. Are other straws more reliable indicators, such as the appointment of Mark Malloch Brown? This has apparently distressed the American administration, because Lord Malloch-Brown has not always been an obedient man. How far might he be relied upon to parrot the necessary untruths so crucial to the conduct of the alliance? The egregious Mr. Bolton has already signalled his displeasure. The appointment was an 'inauspicious beginning', he said.

Another useful indicator of changing Government policy is the abandonment of the sick phraseology of the war on terror, used to describe the various criminal onslaughts of Jihadists in Britain. Undoubtedly the arrangement of explosions in public places generates terror. But it is not a war: wars are conducted between States, and indeed this is not their proudest accomplishment. The explosions to harm the civilian population which have recently been prevented in London and Glasgow, were attempted criminal acts, punishable under the criminal law. Had they been part of a genuine war, then their perpetrators, now arrested, would qualify as prisoners of war and would escape criminal sanction. But their patrons, by contrast, might qualify for bombardment or other military punishment. Not for the first time, Mr. Blair impaled himself on his own heady rhetoric. That he had willing followers does not validate that rhetoric: it merely establishes that foolishness can sometimes be fashionable.

We certainly live in stirring times, and just for a moment it looks as if there might be a window of choice. Should Britain withdraw from the obscene adventure in Iraq, then the political landscape would be profoundly changed. Everyone knows that the British commitment to the war cannot last indefinitely, and must soon be brought to an end. But if it were brought to an end decisively, by resolute action, then the Government would face a real wave of relief and hope. If things meander on, dithering to an exhausted collapse, the military result may well be the same, but the political impact will be very different.

Meantime, even if the dreadful legacy of Blair in Basra and Baghdad is lifting, and it requires an almost superhuman optimism to hope for this, the mutated legacy of Blair in Palestine is only now beginning to show its capacity for harm.

* * *

Mikhail Gorbachev and Helmut Kohl now find themselves securely in history. Tony Blair is about to join them, although they may not find him inspired company. Nonetheless, the story is the thing, and all Blair's peccadilloes may indeed make colourful reading for future generations. The legacy of George Bush II shows its own capacity for harm on an even wider stage. It is unfortunate that the agreements reached by Kohl and Gorbachev have themselves been honoured more securely in the breach than they have in the observance. Lesser men have not hesitated to flout them, even to negate them, and to leave us, therefore, in a more perilous and precarious world.

A careful account of the negotiations between Gorbachev and Kohl has been given by Hannes Adomeit,[1] in a working paper delivered at the Sorbonne in June 2006.

Adomeit points out that a principal objective of Soviet policy before 1990 had been the ousting of the Americans from Europe. It could be argued that this objective was somewhat platonic, but it was certainly at odds with the New Thinking, which saw the *de facto* dissolution of Nato as 'destabilising'. After all, if the Americans gave up their European engagement, what would prevent Bonn from seeking to become a nuclear power? So it is to Gorbachev that we owe the decision to sustain Nato, in order not to 'rupture the world fabric'. But if Germany were to be reunited, did this mean that the unification would bring all Germany into Nato, or would there be some artifice by which this could be avoided, without subtracting the Federal Republic from the American alliance?

Historically, there had been two alliances, so that there was a formal problem of convergence between Nato and the Warsaw Pact. But the Warsaw Treaty was disintegrating, and it became increasingly obvious that it was in no position to take over a negotiating role.

Prime Minister Modrow, from the German Democratic Republic, hoped to obtain a commitment to German neutrality. Then the federation between the GDR and the FRG could be negotiated on the basis of military neutrality between both.[2] Gregor Gysi, at that time the Leader of the East German PDS, presented these arguments at a meeting in Moscow on the 2nd February 1990. Present were

Gorbachev, Yakovlev and Falin. This proposed that a unified Germany should be both neutral and demilitarised, but the Russian news agency, significantly, did not report this latter stipulation. Here was an indication of the fluidity which became a continuous feature of these talks.

This revealed itself when James Baker met with Gorbachev and Shevardnadze a week later on the 8th and 9th of February. During that meeting, Baker volunteered that if Germany were, by consent, to remain part of Nato during the unification process, 'there would be no extension of Nato's jurisdiction for forces of Nato one inch to the east'. Apparently Baker then asked Gorbachev 'whether he would rather see an independent Germany outside of Nato and with no US forces on German soil, or a united Germany tied to Nato but with assurances "that there would be no extension of Nato's current jurisdiction eastward". Gorbachev replied that he was still giving thought to these options … One thing was clear, however: "Any extension of the zone of Nato is unacceptable." "I agree" Baker replied.'

Adomeit chronicles the hesitations and doubts of Gorbachev during this process of negotiation. Should Germany be a member of Nato politically, but stay outside its military organisation? That would give it a status analogous to that chosen by France. Or how could the Atlantic alliance define its jurisdiction to precisely exclude any widening of scope by Nato? Should Germany be completely demilitarised? In the end, Gorbachev agreed with Kohl to let the Germans determine the shape and speed of unification, but left open the question of Germany's alliances.

Then, on the 24th February, Kohl agreed with President Bush I that

> 'a unified Germany should remain a full member of the North Atlantic Treaty Organization, including participation in its military structure. We agreed that US military force should remain stationed in the united Germany and elsewhere in Europe as a continuing guarantor of stability. The chancellor and I are also in agreement that in a unified state, the former territory of the GDR should have a special military status {that} would take into account the legitimate security interests of all interested countries, including those of the Soviet Union.'

The determination of a clear position by the Americans and the Federal Republic was followed by a period of backtracking by Gorbachev, and equivocation by the leaders of the German Democratic Republic. But then Parliamentary Elections in East Germany produced a strong victory for the Conservative parties, which won forty-eight per cent of the popular vote. The PDS gained only sixteen per cent, and the SPD, which had been seen as the likely frontrunner, did only slightly better with twenty-two per cent. Unsurprisingly the Soviet position hardened. But a harder position did not reflect an increase in strength: the contrary is true. In terms of popular support, the position in Germany showed a considerable weakening of Soviet influence. In many other East European countries that weakening was commonly more acute, so that it was increasingly difficult to sustain the Soviet arguments on European stability.

Hannes Adomeit describes a process which is uncomfortably like that of pulling teeth. But yes, Gorbachev did give his consent to Germany's membership in Nato. And yet none of the difficulties involved in that decision can annul the categorical promises that Nato would not begin a runaway advance to the East.

Did all those promises lapse with the fall of Gorbachev? The very great turbulence which accompanied the collapse of the Soviet Union certainly distracted attention from a variety of important strategic matters. Both in Russia and in the United States, people were happy to think about something else, at least for some of the time.

James A. Baker III came forward with what he called a road map for the extension of Nato eastwards, to include 'not only the States of Central and Eastern Europe, but also a democratic Russia'.[3] If Russia were included, any divergence of views would become a matter for internal negotiation rather than military confrontation, he thought. But there was powerful opposition to this proposal from both sides. Many in the West did not wish to dilute what they regarded as their victory in the Cold War, and many in the East were equally sceptical for very different reasons.

Ninety-six per cent of Russians polled during the Kosovo conflict of 1999 thought that Nato's bombardment of Yugoslavia was a crime against humanity, and three-quarters of these people thought that there was nothing to stop Nato from becoming involved in Russian affairs just as it had in Yugoslavia.

In July 2002, when that issue seemed to lie more quietly among the world's unsolved problems, President Putin took up the question of Nato again, shortly before a summit with President Bush II. He challenged the Western alliance either to enrol Russia or to disband, calling Nato 'a Cold War relic that will only continue to sow the seeds of suspicion in Europe as long as it excludes its one time enemy'.

James Baker's liberal approach to this problem has not aroused any feverish mood of support: in his article in the winter issue of the *Washington Quarterly*, 2002, Baker downplayed his call to say: 'My point ... is not that Russia should be admitted to Nato today, but that Russia should be eligible to apply for admission with a firm commitment to membership if and when Russia has substantially satisfied ... five explicit criteria'. Since 2002 the willingness of the Russians to sit any such test has markedly diminished. In one area after another, relations have somewhat deteriorated, and in some areas the deterioration has been marked. Many if not most Russians will insist that the tests should all be applied the other way. They see heavy intervention by the United States and some of its more ideological NGOs in what they regard as 'the near abroad'. Certainly, the Rose Revolution in Georgia and the Orange Revolution in Ukraine followed a pattern already established in Belgrade after the cessation of those hostilities.

And all the while, contrary to all those positive assurances during the negotiations about the future of Germany, Nato continuously expanded.[4] It had already grown into Eastern Europe before the Yugoslav war, and it followed that war by a surge of new adhesions. Just as significant was the transformation of the declared role of the organisation: time was when actions were supposed to be 'in area', and would be precluded 'out of area'. 'Everything is (now) Nato's area', said Daniel Fried, the Assistant Secretary of State for European and Eurasian Affairs in April 2007.

But not only is the world Nato's new oyster, but the range of questions which it might address has been conspicuously widened. Today, Russia is deemed to be energy rich, and Europe is energy poor. Any threat to cut the energy resources of Nato members is deemed by some of them to provide an excuse for joint action, up to and including military action. It would be very strange indeed if the Russians could view such developments with equanimity.

Nato fleets are already deployed in the Eastern Mediterranean, in the Gulf, and in the waters around the Horn of Africa. Denmark is capable under this agency of lurching into war against Syria. We have always been cautious in reacting to the warlike noises which the Americans have made against Iran. But we have been hearing these noises and noticing that military planning can seem more audacious and less nuanced than many of the politicians would like.

In July 2007, we clearly face a moment of choice in Iraq, with the war steadily losing support among American voters, and the chaos refusing to yield to any number of new American forces. And the Americans are short of new forces. America's crisis will renew the crises that afflict the different constituents of Nato.

It is highly doubtful whether embryonic peace movements of this tortured world will ever be able to find an effective focus for their activities, until they are able to call an end to Nato and its adventures, and a beginning to the effective regeneration of international co-operation. This is a very big agenda: but the longer we defer our approach to it, the more difficult it will become.

Ken Coates

References

1. Hannes Adomeit: **Gorbachev's Consent to Unified Germany's Membership in NATO**. Paper delivered to the Conference on 'Europe and the End of the Cold War', at the Université de Sorbonne, Paris, June 15th-17th 2006, revised November 1st 2006. A Working Paper of the Research Unit Russia/CIS Stiftung Wissenschaft und Politik German Institute for International and Security Affairs.
2. Ibid, p. 5.
3. *Russia in Nato?* **The Washington Quarterly**, Winter 2002, pp. 95-103.
4. Unified Germany acceded to the Nato Treaty (Treaty of Washington) in October 1990. The Czech Republic, Hungary and Poland joined in 1999. Bulgaria, Estonia, Latvia, Lithuania, Romania, Slovakia and Slovenia joined in March 2004.

45 minute threat:
'I realised something was wrong' – Major

John Major was interviewed by Elinor Goodman on the BBC on 28 April 2007, from which this excerpt is taken.

Goodman: When the world outside became aware of sofa government was over Iraq. Can you understand how Tony Blair would have got the intelligence so wrong? Do you think it was a deliberate misuse of intelligence or a misunderstanding of it?

Major: I must be very careful here because I can't be certain. I can only tell you I was Prime Minister during the first Iraq war, and whenever I said anything about Iraq, I always said less than I knew and only what I was absolutely confident of. And I supported the Government's position on Iraq because I assumed that was a principle that still applied. I realised something was wrong that famous weekend when there were so many stories about Saddam Hussein having a missile that would hit us in 45 minutes. I knew that he could not, and did not, and that was untrue. And I waited the whole weekend for Downing Street …

Goodman: How did you know that?

Major: I did use to get a lot of security briefings during the period I was there, and I had some after I was there as well …

Goodman: See you'd seen the same intelligence that he was making that assessment on?

Major: Oh but years out of date. But it was inconceivable during that period that Saddam Hussein, that Iraq, had moved on to have a missile capable of hitting the United Kingdom in 45 minutes from Iraq.

I waited the whole weekend for Downing Street to correct that story, and they didn't correct that story which I knew to be wrong. And from then onwards I looked with a much more sceptical eye at everything that was said about Iraq.

But let me add one further point. I do not know what information was on the Prime Minister's desk when he made his decisions. Let me make that perfectly clear. So everything I say, I say with that caveat. There may, may, have been something that I didn't know that persuaded him to speak as he did …

Stones

John Berger

This excerpt is taken from John Berger's new book, Hold Everything Dear – Dispatches on Survival and Resistance, *published by Verso Books (£12.99). It is reprinted here with grateful acknowledgements.*

(June 2003)

Eqbal Ahmed was, I think, a man who saw life whole. He was cunning, quick, had little time to spare for fools, loved cooking, and was the opposite of an opportunist – of somebody who fragments life. I once wrote an account of his childhood in Bihar at the time of the partition of India and Pakistan. It was a version on paper of what he told me one night in a bar in Amsterdam. He asked me when he read it to change his name. Which I did. The story was about what made him decide, at the age of seventeen, to become a revolutionary. Now he's dead, I return his name to him.

Influenced by the writings of Franz Fanon – and particularly by *The Damned of the Earth* – he became deeply involved in several liberation struggles, including that of the Palestinians. I remember him talking to me about Jenin. Towards the end of his life, Eqbal set up a freethinking university in Pakistan named after the great fifteenth-century philosopher Ibn Khaldun, who imagined the discipline of sociology before it existed.

Eqbal learnt early on that life inevitably leads to separations. Everybody recognized this before the category of the tragic was discarded as garbage. Eqbal, though, knew and accepted the tragic. And, consequently, he spent much prodigious energy on forging links – of friendship, political solidarity, military loyalty, shared poetry, hospitality – links which had a chance of surviving after the inevitable separations. I still remember the meals he cooked.

I didn't expect to encounter Eqbal in Ramallah. Although, oddly, the first book I picked up and opened there had a photo of him on the third page. No, I wasn't looking for him. Yet he had been beside me when I decided to visit the city, and he left me a message which I saw like an SMS on the tiny screen of my imagination.

Look at the stones! it said.

O.K., I replied, the stones, in my own way.

Certain trees – particularly the mulberries and medlars – still tell the story of how long ago, in another life, before the *Nakbah,* Ramallah was, for the well-off, a town of leisure and ease, a place to retreat to from nearby Jerusalem during the hot summers, a resort. The *Nakbah* refers to the 'catastrophe' of 1948 when ten thousand Palestinians were killed and 700,000 were forced to leave their country.

Long ago, newly married couples planted roses in Ramallah gardens as an augury for their future life together. The alluvial soil suited the roses.

Today there is not a wall in the town centre of Ramallah, now the capital of the Palestinian Authority, which is not covered with the photographs of the dead, taken when alive and now reprinted as small posters. The dead are the martyrs of the Second Intifada which began in September 2000. The martyrs include all those killed by the Israeli army and settlers, and those who decided to sacrifice themselves in suicidal counter-attacks. These faces transform the desultory street walls into something as intimate as a wallet of private papers and pictures. The wallet has a pocket for the magnetic ID card issued by the Israeli security services and without which no Palestinian can travel even a few kilometres, and another pocket for eternity. Around the posters, the walls are scarred with bullet and shrapnel marks.

There is an old woman, who might be the grandmother in several wallets. There are boys in their early teens, there are many fathers. Listening to the stories of how they met their death, one is reminded of what poverty is about. Poverty forces the hardest choices which lead to almost nothing. Poverty is living with that *almost.*

Most of the boys, whose faces are on the walls, were born in refugee camps, as poor as shantytowns. They left school early to earn money for the family or help the father with his job, if he had one. A few dreamt of becoming wizard soccer players. A fair number of them made catapults of carved wood, twined rope and twisted leather for hurling stones at the Occupying Army.

Any comparison between the weapons involved in these confrontations returns us to what poverty is about. On one hand Apache and Cobra helicopters, Fl6s, Abrams tanks, Humvee jeeps, electronic surveillance systems, tear gas; on the other hand catapults, slingshots, mobile telephones, badly used Kalashnikovs and mostly handmade explosives. The enormity of the contrast reveals something which I can feel between these grief-stricken walls but which I cannot put a name to. If I was an Israeli soldier, however well-armed I was, I might finally be frightened of this something. Perhaps it's what the poet Mourid Barghouti noticed: 'Living people grow old but martyrs grow younger.'

Three stories from the walls.

Husni Al-Nayjar, fourteen years old. He worked helping his father, who was a welder. Whilst flinging stones, he was shot dead with a bullet to the head. In his photo he gazes calmly and unwaveringly into the middle distance.

Abdelhamid Kharti, thirty-four years old. Painter and writer. When young, he had trained as a medical nurse. He volunteered to join a medical emergency unit for rescuing and taking care of the wounded. His corpse was found near a checkpoint, after a night when there had been no confrontations. His fingers had been cut off. A thumb was hanging loose. An arm, a hand and his jaw were broken: There were twenty bullets in his body.

Muhammad Al-Durra, twelve years old, lived in the Breij Camp. He was returning home with his father across the Netzarim checkpoint in Gaza and they were ordered to get out of their vehicle. Soldiers were already shooting. The two of them took immediate cover behind a cement wall. The father waved to show they were there and was shot in the hand. A little later Muhammad was shot in the foot. The father now shielded his son with his own body. More bullets hit both, and the boy was killed. Doctors removed eight bullets from the father's body, but he remained paralyzed as a consequence of the wounds and could no longer work, remaining unemployed. Because the incident happened to be filmed, the story is told and retold across the world.

I want to do a drawing for Abdelhamid Kharti. Very early in the morning we go to the village of Ain Kinya and beyond it there's a Bedouin encampment, near a wadi. The sun is not yet hot. The goats and sheep are grazing more or less between the tents. I've chosen to draw the hills looking eastwards. I sit on a rock near a small blackish tent. I have only a notebook and this pen. There's a discarded plastic mug on the earth and it gives me the idea of fetching some water from the trickle of the spring to mix, when necessary, with my ink.

After I've been drawing for a while, a young man (every person in the camp has of course noticed me) approaches, undoes the entrance to the tent behind me, enters and comes out holding up a decrepit white plastic stool which, he indicates, might be more comfortable than the rock. I guess that before he found it, it must have been thrown out into the street by some pastry shop or ice-cream parlour. I thank him.

And sitting on this customer's stool in the Bedouin camp, as the sun gets hotter and the frogs in the almost dry riverbed begin to croak, I go on drawing.

On a hilltop, a few kilometres to the left, is an Israeli settlement. It looks military, as if it were part of a weapon designed for quick handling. Yet it's small and faraway.

The near limestone hill facing me has the form of a gigantic sleeping animal's head, the rocks scattered on it like burrs in its matted hair. Suddenly frustrated by my lack of pigment, I pour water from the mug on to the dust at my feet, dip my finger into the mud and smear colour across the drawing of the animal's head. The sun is hot now. A mule brays. I turn the pages of the notebook to begin another and another. Nothing looks finished. When the young man eventually returns, he wants to see my drawings.

I hold up the open notebook. He smiles. I turn a page. He points. Ours, he says, our dust! He's pointing at my finger, not the drawing.

Then we both look at the hill.

I am among not the conquered but the defeated, whom the victors fear. The time of the victors is always short and that of the defeated unaccountably long. Their space is different too. Everything in this limited land is a question of space, and the victors have understood this. The stranglehold they maintain is first and foremost spatial. It is applied, illegally and in defiance of international law, through the checkpoints, through the destruction of ancient roads, through the new by-passes strictly reserved for Israeli settlers, through the fortress hilltop settlements, which are really surveillance and control points of the surrounding plateaux, through the curfew which obliges people to stay indoors night and day until it is lifted. During the invasion of Ramallah last year, the curfew lasted six weeks, with a 'lifting' of a couple of hours on certain days for shopping. There was not even enough time to bury those who died in their beds.

The dissenting Israeli architect Eyal Weizman has pointed out in a courageous book that this total terrestrial domination begins in the drawings of district-planners and architects. The violence begins long before the arrival of the tanks and jeeps. He talks of a 'politics of verticality', whereby the defeated even when 'at home' are being literally *overseen* and undermined

The effect of this on daily life is relentless. As soon as somebody one morning says to himself 'I'll go and see –' he has to stop short and check how many crossings of barriers the 'outing' is likely to involve. The space of the simplest everyday decisions is hobbled, with its foreleg tethered to its hind leg.

In addition, because the barriers change unpredictably from day to day, experience of time is hobbled. Nobody knows how long it will take this morning to get to work, to go and see Mother, to attend a class, to consult the doctor, nor, having done these things, how long it will take to get back home. The trip, in either direction, may take thirty minutes or four hours, or the route may be categorically shut off by soldiers with their loaded submachine guns.

The Israeli government claims that they are obliged to take these measures to combat terrorism. The claim is a feint. The true aim of the stranglehold is to destroy the indigenous population's sense of temporal and spatial continuity so that they either leave or become indentured servants. And it's here that the dead help the living to resist. It's here that men and women make their decision to become martyrs. The stranglehold inspires the terrorism it purports to be fighting.

A small road of stones, negotiating boulders, descending into a valley south of Ramallah. Sometimes it winds between olive groves of old trees, a number of them perhaps dating from Roman times. This rocky track (very hard on any car) is the only means of access for Palestinians to their nearby village. The original asphalt road, forbidden to them now, is reserved for Israelis in the settlements. I walk ahead because all my life I have found it more tiring to walk slowly. I spot a red flower amongst the shrubs and stop to pick it. Later I learn it is called Adonis Aestivalis. Its red is very intense and its life, the botanical book says, brief.

Baha shouts to warn me not to head towards the high hill on my left. If they spot someone approaching, he shouts, they shoot.

I try to calculate the distance: less than a kilometre. A couple of hundred metres away in the unrecommended direction I spot a tethered mule and horse. I take them as a guarantee and I walk there.

When I arrive, two boys – aged about eleven and eight – are working alone in a field. The younger one is filling watering-cans from a barrel buried in the earth. The care with which he does so, not spilling a drop, shows how precious the water is. The elder boy takes the full can and carefully climbs down to a ploughed plot where he is watering plants. Both of them are barefoot.

The one watering beckons to me and proudly shows me the rows of several hundred plants on the plot. Some I recognize: tomatoes, aubergines, cucumbers. They must have been planted during the last week. They're still small, searching for water. One plant I don't recognize and he notices this. Big light, he says. Melon? Shumaam! We laugh. His laughing eyes fixed on me don't waver. (I think of Husni Al-Nayjar.) We are both – God knows why – living at the same moment. He takes me down the rows to show me how much he has watered. At one moment we pause, look around and glance at the settlement with its defensive walls and red roofs. As he points with his chin in its direction there is a kind of derision in his gesture, a derision which he wants to share with me, like his pride in watering. A derision which gives way to a grin – as if we had both agreed to piss at the same moment at the same spot.

Later we walk back towards the rocky road. He picks some short mint and hands me a bunch. Its pungent freshness is like a draught of cold water, water colder than that in the watering-can. We are going towards the horse and mule. The horse, unsaddled, has a halter with reins but neither bridle nor bit, He wants to demonstrate to me something more impressive than an imaginary piss. He leaps onto the horse whilst his brother reassures the mule, and almost instantly he is galloping, bareback, down the road from which I came. The horse has six legs, four of its own and two belonging to its rider, and the boy's hands control all six, He rides with the experience of several lifetimes. When he returns, he is grinning and, for the first time, looks shy,

I rejoin Baha and the others, who are a kilometre away. They are talking to a man, who is the boy's uncle, and who is likewise watering plants which have been recently bedded out. The sun is going down and the light is changing. The brownish yellow earth, which is darker where it has been watered, is now the primary colour of the whole landscape. He is using the last of the water in the bottom of a 500-litre dark blue plastic barrel.

On the surface of the blue barrel eleven patches – like those used for mending punctures but larger – have been carefully stuck. The man will explain to me that this is how he repaired the barrel after a gang from the settlement of Halamish, the settlement with red roofs, came one night, when they knew the water containers were full of spring rain, and slashed them with knives. Another barrel, lying on the terrace below, was irreparable. Further off on the same terrace stands the gnarled stump of an olive tree, which, to judge by its girth, must have been several hundred, perhaps a thousand, years old.

A few nights ago, the uncle says, they cut it down with a chain saw.

I quote again from Mourid Barghouti: 'For the Palestinian, olive oil is the gift of the traveller, the comfort of the bride, the reward of autumn, the boast of the storeroom and the wealth of the family across centuries.'

Later, I find a poem by Zakaria Mohammed called The Bit. It talks about a black horse without a bridle which has blood dripping from its lips. With Zakaria's horse too there is a boy, astonished by the blood.

> *What is the black horse chewing?*
> *he asks,*
> *What does it chew?*
> *The black horse*
> *is biting*
> *a bit forged from steel*
> *a bit of memory*
> *to be champed on*
> *champed on until death.*

If the boy who gave me the short mint was seven years older, it wouldn't be hard to imagine why he joined Hamas, ready to sacrifice his life.

The weight of the concrete slabs and fallen masonry of Arafat's wrecked compound in the centre of Ramallah has taken on a symbolic gravity. Not, however, in the way the Israeli commanders imagined. Smashing the Muqata with Arafat and his company in it was for them a public demonstration of his humiliation, just as in the private apartments which the army systematically raided and searched, the tomato ketchup smeared on to clothes, furniture and walls was a private warning of worse to come,

Arafat still represents the Palestinians more faithfully perhaps than any other world leader represents his people. Not democratically but tragically. Hence the gravity. Due to the many errors committed by the PLO, with him at its head, and due to the equivocations of the surrounding Arab states, he has no room left for political manoeuvre. He has ceased to be a political leader. Yet he remains defiantly here. Nobody believes in him. And many would give their lives for him. How is this? No longer a politician, Arafat has become a rubble mountain, but a mountain of the homeland.

I have never seen such a light before. It comes down from the sky in a strangely regular way, for it makes no distinction between what is distant and what is close. The difference between far and near is one of scale, never of colour, texture or precision. And this affects the way you place yourself, it affects your sense of being here. The land arranges itself around you, rather than confronting you. It's the opposite of Arizona. Instead of beckoning, it recommends never leaving.

And so I am here, a figure in a dream that some of my ancestors in Poland,

Galicia and the Austro-Hungarian Empire must have nurtured, and spoken about for at least two centuries. And here I unhesitatingly identify myself with the just cause and the pain of those whom the state of Israel (and cousins of mine) are afflicting to a degree that is tragically totalitarian.

Riad, who is a teacher of carpentry, has gone to fetch his drawings to show me. We are sitting in the garden of his father's house. The father with his white horse is harrowing the field opposite, When Riad comes back he's carrying the drawings like a file taken out of an old-fashioned metal filing cabinet. He walks slowly and the chickens move out of his way more slowly. He sits opposite me and hands me the drawings one by one. They are drawn with a hard-lead pencil, from memory and with great patience. Stroke upon stroke in the evenings after work, until the blacks become as black as he wants, the greys remaining silvery. They are on quite large sheets of paper.

A drawing of a water pitcher. A drawing of his mother. A drawing of a house which was destroyed, of windows that gave on to rooms which have gone.

When I at last put the drawings down, an older man, with the enduring face of a peasant, addresses me. It sounds as if you know about chickens, he says. When a hen falls ill, she stops laying. Little to be done. One day though, she wakes up and feels Death approaching. One day she realizes she's going to die, and what happens? She begins laying again, and nothing but death can stop her. We are like that hen.

The checkpoints function as interior frontiers imposed on the Occupied territories, yet they do not resemble any normal frontier-post. They are constructed and manned in such a way that everyone who passes is reduced to the status of an unwanted refugee.

Impossible to underestimate the importance for the stranglehold of Decor, used as a constant reminder of who are the victors and who should recognize that they are the conquered. Palestinians have to undergo, often several times a day, the humiliation of playing the part of refugees in their own homeland.

Everyone crossing has to walk on foot past the checkpoint, where soldiers, loaded guns at the ready, pick on whoever they wish to 'check'. No vehicles can cross. The traditional road has been destroyed. The new obligatory 'route' has been strewn with boulders, stones and other minor obstacles. Consequently, all, even the fit, have to hobble across.

The sick and elderly are pushed in wooden boxes on four wheels (boxes originally made for carting vegetables in the market) by young men, who earn a small living like this. They hand each passenger a cushion to soften the bumps. They listen to their stories. They always know the latest news. (The barriers alter every day.) They offer advice, they lament and they are proud of the little aid they offer. They are perhaps the nearest to a Chorus of the tragedy.

Some 'commuters' walk with the aid of a stick, some even on crutches. Everything which normally would be in the boot of a vehicle has to be hoicked across in bundles carried by hand or on the back. The distance of a crossing can change overnight from anything between 300 metres and 1.5 kilometres.

Palestinian couples, except for certain more sophisticated young ones, generally observe in public the decorum of a certain distance. At the checkpoints couples of all ages hold hands as they cross, searching with each step for a foothold, and calculating exactly the right pace for hobbling past the pointing guns, neither too fast – hurrying can arouse suspicion, nor too slow – hesitation can provoke a 'game' for relieving the guards' chronic boredom.

The vindictiveness of many (not all) Israeli soldiers is particular. It has little to do with the cruelty which Euripedes described and lamented, for here the confrontation is not between equals, but between the all-powerful and the apparently powerless. Yet this power of the powerful is accompanied by a furious frustration: the discovery that, despite all their weapons, their power has an inexplicable limit.

I want to change some euros for shekels – the Palestinians have no currency of their own. I walk down the Main Street passing many small shops, and, occasionally, a man sitting on a chair, where there would once have been a pavement before the invasion of the tanks. In their hands these men hold wads of bank notes. I approach a young one and say I want to change 100 euros. (For that amount one could buy in one of the gold shops a small bracelet for a child.) He consults a child's pocket calculator and hands me several hundred shekels.

I walk on. A boy who, age-wise, might be the brother of the girl with the imaginary golden bracelet, holds out some chewing gum for me to buy. He is from one of the two refugee camps in Ramallah. I buy. He's also selling plastic covers for the magnetic ID cards in the wallet. His scowl suggests I buy all the chewing gum. I do.

Half an hour passes and I'm in the vegetable market. A man is selling garlic the size of electric light-bulbs. There are many people close together. Somebody taps me on the shoulder. I turn round. It's the money-changer. I gave you, he says, fifty shekels too little, here they are. I take five notes of ten. You were easy to find, he adds. I thank him.

The expression in his eyes as he looks at me reminds me of an old woman I have seen the day before. An expression of great attention to the moment. Calm and considered, as if it could conceivably be the last moment.

The money-changer then turns and begins his long walk back to the chair.

I met the old woman in the village of Kobar. The house was concrete, unfinished and sparse. On the walls of the bare salon were framed photographs of her nephew, Marwan Barghouti. Marwan as a boy, an adolescent, a man of forty. Today he is in an Israeli prison. If he survives, he is one of the few political leaders of the Fatah with whom it will be essential to consult concerning any solid peace agreement.

Whilst we were drinking lemon juice and the Aunt was making coffee, her grandchildren came out into the garden: two boys aged about seven and nine. The younger one is called Homeland and the elder one Struggle. They ran around in every direction and would suddenly stop, looking intently at one another, as if they were hiding behind something and peering out to see whether the other one had spotted them. Then they would move again to another invisible hide-out. A game they had invented and played together many times.

The third child was four years old. On his face were red and white daubs as on a clown's, and he stood apart like a clown, wistful, jokey, unsure when it would be over. He had chickenpox and knew he should not approach visitors.

When it came to saying good-bye, the Aunt held my hand, and in her eyes, there was this same special expression of attention to the moment.

If two people are laying a tablecloth on a table, they glance at one another to check the placing of the cloth. Imagine the table is the world and the cloth the lives of those we have to save. Such was the expression.

A small brass bowl called a Fear Cup. Engraved with filigree geometric patterns and some verses from the Koran arranged in the form of a flower. Fill it with water and leave it outside under the stars for a night. Then drink the water whilst praying that it will alleviate the pain and cure you. For many sicknesses the Fear Cup is clearly less effective than a course of antibiotics. But a bowl of water which has reflected the time of the stars, the same water from which every living thing was made, as is said in the Koran, may help to resist the stranglehold ...

Two weeks after leaving Ramallah I am in Finistère in north-west France, looking out to sea. The contrast of climate and vegetation cannot be greater. The only thing in common is an abundance of brambles – *toot il alliq*. The Finistère coast is green with ferns, until it falls to the rocks. And it is broken into countless small islands by the impact of an ocean, which changes its colour every half hour. The western coast of Europe from Cornwall to Spanish Galicia has been named Land's End. Here the land ends in ferns and islets like boulders.

I have come to see the most ancient built monument in the world, constructed a thousand years before the earliest pyramids. It too was constructed as a funerary monument. What I'm looking at, Eqbal, is a pile of stones. The guide books call it a cairn.

Yet it's far more than a cairn; it's a highly articulated sculpture. Every forty centimetres of it has been, as it were, hand-written. It's over seventy metres long, about twenty-five metres wide and eight or ten metres tall, and in each direction each stone joins the following one intentionally, as if the stones were hand-written words.

Imagine the deck of a ship. She's heading north-east to get out of the bay of Morlaix, and then she can go west towards America. This ship with her Homeric prow (local legend has it that Odysseus passed by this coast on his way to Cork), this ship is made of stones, and naturally she is married to the earth!

According to the carbon datings, she was built at least six thousand years ago, on two separate occasions. First the stern was made with greenish metamorphic dolerite stones, such as abound along the coast with its acid earth beneath the ferns. Then, a century or two later, the prow was added, made mostly with oat-coloured granite, which came from the little island of Sterec.

There was a third construction which may have been a second ship of death, but this was utterly destroyed in the 1950s, when the whole site, which had long since been overgrown and covered with earth, was being exploited as a quarry, and the stones used for making gravel.

Archaeologists deduce that each part of the ship, on the two occasions, was built within a few months. And this, given the labour involved, presumes that a whole settler community of several hundred people worked together on it.

Most of the stones are the size and weight of what a strong man might carry between his two arms. There are also smaller ones, small as a fist, for filling in the recalcitrant spaces left in the otherwise perfect fitting together of the larger ones.

The ship's decks are smooth, not cobbled. And there are a few megaliths, taller than a man, used as lintels over the entrances to passageways, or, sometimes, as a table-roof for vaulted chambers. On the lower deck, twenty-two dry-stone passages, from port and starboard, lead to eleven vaulted cabins, where the dead were placed.

I follow one such passage, which is like a sentence leading to a centre, and here, in the half-destroyed sanctuary, I gaze at the stones corbelling out. They are the same as millions of other stones on the beaches of this coast, except that here, they speak and are eloquent, due to their arrangement.

Chaos perhaps has its reasons, but chaos is dumb. From the human capacity to arrange, to place, come language and communication. The word *place* is both verb and noun. The capacity of arrangement and the capacity to recognize and name a site. Aren't both inseparable in their origin from the human need to respect and defend their dead?

A strange comparison occurs to me. What inspired hundreds of people to work together for several months to build this ship of stones, is perhaps quite close to what inspires kids in Palestine to hurl stones at the tanks of an occupying army.

Hold Everything Dear, ISBN 978 1 84467 138 0 (www.versobooks.com)

Eyeless in Gaza

The liberation of Alan Johnston and the imprisonment of Gaza

Daily in the common Prison
    else enjoyn'd me,
Where I a Prisoner chain'd,
    scarce freely draw
The air imprison'd also,
    close and damp,
Unwholsom draught …
            John Milton,
            Samson Agonistes

Usamah Hamden
Michael Ancram MP
Jonathan Lehrle
Mark Perry

This is an edited transcript of a discussion with Hamas's representative in Lebanon, which took place in Beirut on 19 June. The participants' biographical notes are appended at the end.

Michael Ancram: Good to see you. Lots has happened since we last met.[1] I guess you have been busy, Gaza has been interesting, I'm keen to hear what has been going on. How do you think things will go?

Usamah Hamdan: I will start from the Mecca Agreement. At Mecca there were three important points. The first one was on the National Unity Government; the second point covered the reform of the security services and called for a new security plan for the Palestinian territories, and the third point was on the reform of the PLO and the new political arrangements inside the Palestinian political body. That means the relations within the PLO itself, the relations between the PLO and the Palestinian Authority, the internal Palestinian relations.[2] And we [in the Hamas movement] went back to Gaza and within one month there was the formation of the National Unity Government. We started talking about security. There was a security plan that was put forward and that was endorsed by the government and that was then endorsed by Abu Mazen himself as President.[3]

When we started to apply that [the security plan] on the ground we faced an important problem – which was that the main General in the security service failed to apply and rejected

---

1. Ancram, Lehrle, Perry and Conflicts Forum Founder and Director, Alastair Crooke, had a private meeting with Hamdan in Beirut during the first week of April, 2007.
2. This was stated in order of priority. That is to say: at Mecca, the parties agreed that the overriding issue was for Fatah and for Hamas to agree to a security programme prior to shaping any political agreements. The two parties said that they would present their programmes for a security arrangement in the first weeks after the conclusion of the Mecca Agreement.
3. The security plan adopted by Hamas called for a single security service comprised of elements of the Hamas armed militia integrated with elements of the standing Fatah militia security services so that there would be a single security service acting under the lead of an interior minister accountable to an elected Palestinian president. Disarmament of independent militias, it was believed by the Hamas leadership, could go forward once the security plan was agreed to.

this plan. That was General Rashid Abu Shabak.[4] He ordered all the security officers not to receive the Interior Minister without permission.[5] So we were not able to make any progress. We were not able to go anywhere and the Interior Minister was not able to order the security service to implement the security plan that was agreed to. The Interior Minister was not able to order any security service to apply the plan.[6]

So because of these difficulties we talked directly to Abu Mazen in April in Cairo, and it was a frank talk about this plan which was endorsed by himself, and we insisted that the plan that was agreed be implemented. But he did not promise to do anything. He just said, 'I will talk with Mr Mohammad Dahlan and then I will give you an answer, and this answer will be inside the territories.' [That is: 'I will give you the answer in the West Bank or Gaza and not during a meeting in Cairo.'] He [Abu Mazen] went to Gaza. He had a meeting with the Interior Minister and he told him, 'I consulted with Mohammad Dahlan and he rejected to apply that [agreed to security plan.] So we reached an end point, we reached a closed point in the security plan. At the same time there was another security plan, which was generated by the Americans, you know [Lt. General Keith Dayton], and the Palestinian Mr. Dahlan and some of our neighbours.

This plan (I think a part of it was published) and all the people knew about it – the politicians knew about it – I think you have a copy of this plan.[7] This plan calls for the establishment of a new security force taken from the Presidential Guard. It

---

4. Rashid Abu Shabak was named by Palestinian Authority President Mahmoud Abbas as the head of P.A. Preventive Security for the West Bank and Gaza on 28 April 2005. A close associate of Mohammad Dahlan, Shabak gained his reputation as a tough commander by identifying and turning over collaborators for execution to the security services. However, his reputation is mixed, at best. For instance, he arrested Akram Muhammad al-Zatma for identifying the whereabouts of Hamas leader Saleh Shahedeh (who, along with his family, was killed) to the Israelis – though it is likely that Zatma, who was executed, was innocent of the charges. Shabak's number two was Samir al-Mashharawi, a Fatah official close to the Central Committee, deployed by Abu Mazen to help Shabak. In the wake of the Hamas parliamentary victory in January 2006, Mashharawi was given responsibility for a series of street confrontations through March, April and May of 2006 that pitted Fatah al-Aqsa Martyrs Brigade cadre against the Popular Resistance Committees – competitors with Fatah for power in Gaza.
5. Rashid Abu Shabak's line-of-command is to the President through the head of the National Security Council. The head of the National Security Council is Mohammad Dahlan. The Interior Minister at the time of the controversy over the security plan was Hani al-Qawasmeh. Mr. Qawasmeh threatened to resign several times over Mr. Abu Mazen's refusal to accept the agreed-to security plan, telling Mr. Abu Mazen that Mohammad Dahlan was thwarting the implementation of the plan. His resignation was refused twice before being accepted on 14 May.
6. As the head of the Preventive Security Services, Rashid Abu Shabak takes orders from the head of the National Security Council. The head of the National Security Council is Mohammad Dahlan. Mr. Dahlan reports directly to Palestinian President Mahmoud Abbas. The Fatah-only Preventive Security Services – according to the *Washington Post* – were set up under Mohammad Dahlan to counter the forces of the Executive Services – the Hamas militia – and were comprised of 6,000 officers and enlisted Fatah personnel as of June 1 of 2007. The numbers are uncertain, but the total numbers of Preventive Security Services and Presidential Guard personnel answering solely to Mohammad Dahlan are thought to be between 16,000 and 20,000 persons. None of them belong to Hamas. The position of Hamas has always been that their 6,000 man "Executive Force" should be integrated into the security services.
7. The plan was published in the Jordanian weekly newspaper, *Al-Majd,* and detailed in an article in *Asia Times* entitled, 'Document Details US Plan to Sink Hamas'.

was supposed to train 20,000 soldiers and they were to be trained in Jordan, Egypt, the UK, the US and in Russia. This was a complete plan and the budget for this plan was about $1.27bn dollars and we followed that up. In Cairo there was training for 500 [Palestinians] at that time – in April. They were talking about training up more than 5,000 at the end October and in Jordan they were talking about training about 4,000 and outside in the West they were talking about training about 700 officers. They will collect the other members from the security service.[8]

So they were closing the road for the national security plan and they were having their own security plan. [They were using these plans as a pretext] to give themselves some time.[9] They [Fatah] were undermining their own [National Unity] Government and undermining the security plan which we were working on. In order to make the situation more difficult they started disturbing the security in Gaza by some robberies and killings and by supporting some drug mobs and finally the kidnapping of some people, including the journalist Alan Johnston – who was kidnapped by some members of the [Dagmoush] family, who were directly connected to Mohammad Dahlan.[10]

At this time, in May, we visited Egypt and we talked frankly about what was happening on the ground and we told them [Abu Mazen and other members of the Fatah leadership]: 'From the beginning of March until the end of May those forces [of Dahlan's Preventive Security Services] kidnapped and assassinated 40 members from Hamas. Those kidnapped were not militants. Most of them were

---

8. At one point the US and Jordan considered arming and retraining the 'Badr Brigade', a stay-behind unit of the Palestine Liberation Army in Jordan and deploying it to the West Bank. Israel would not agree to the deployment.
9. It has been reliably reported that the Mr. Omar Suleiman, the Egyptian General Intelligence Chief, was working on behalf of Saudi Arabia to make certain that the security plan was implemented. After a period of paralysis in April, Suleiman planned for a number of meetings between the groups in Cairo in May. But throughout May and into early June, Suleiman was becoming impatient with the lack of progress of both sides in implementing a viable security plan, despite the pressure he was putting on them. As violence mounted in Gaza, Suleiman became increasingly disturbed by attempts to undermine what he viewed as attempts to create stability in Gaza – which would endanger Egyptian assets in the Gaza Strip. During the first week of June, Suleiman convened a meeting of the parties in Cairo to address these incidents. According to an article in the authoritative *Al-Ahram Weekly*: 'The Egypt-Fatah-Hamas meeting ought to conclude in agreement on three issues – the commitment of both sides to work towards a firm end to mutual incitement, either in respectively controlled media or mosques; the effective execution of a detailed plan to collect uncontrolled arms within each group, especially those in the hands of second and third cadres leaders; and firm enforcement of the decisions of the leadership of both factions'. Hamas came with two other demands – first, that Egypt control the actions of Mohammad Dahlan and Rashid Abu Shabak and that the arming of Fatah by the United States and friendly Arab governments be suspended. The talks did not proceed: Fatah officials said they would not meet with Hamas officials in Cairo and cancelled their attendance at the meetings.
10. The Dagmoush family of southern Gaza is a large criminal clan headed by 28-year-old Mumtaz Dagmoush. The family is involved in car theft, arms smuggling and extortion. It has been used in the past as a means for Fatah to spread its control through the Gaza Strip during the Israeli occupation – providing a natural cover for fighters and political figures wanted by the Israelis. 'The Army of Islam' – the group that was holding Alan Johnston – is simply one, albeit radical, arm of the family. Parts of the family have provided support for the emerging Popular Resistance Committees. Mohammad Dahlan's ties to the family are well known: Dahlan's base of support is in Khan Yunis, where he was born and raised, and where the Dagmoushes have powerful influence. The Dagmoush clan is implicated in the kidnapping, last year, of four British citizens.

civilians. Some of them were not only civilians, they were working on public issues and it was clear that some of them were students, some of them were engineers.' But they continued assassinating the people. And you don't want to investigate. Samir Medhoun[11] appeared on Palestinian TV and he said 'well I was responsible for burning 20 houses of Hamas people. I am responsible for killing this man and that man.' He named four people he assassinated. So we talked to Abu Mazen and we said 'you have to arrest him, you have to take him to court' and he said 'I'll try to do something.' Finally we discovered that he was staying in his house – in Abu Mazen's house.[12]

So it was clear what the problem was: this group [the Preventive Security Services] were working on their own agenda. I don't want to say they were connected to the Israelis or the Americans, they were working on their own agenda, which was against the national agenda.[13] Abu Mazen was supposed to make a decision. But I believe he could not do that. This is the best thing if you want to say more than this, he may be involved in this. I prefer to say he could not do anything. He knew those people were supported by the Americans and the Israelis. And he could not do anything against them.

Michael Ancram: Was Dahlan involved with them?

Usamah Hamdan: Yes, Dahlan was involved with them. I want to add one more thing which is important. Some senior advisors working with Abu Mazen went to Europe and to the United States and some of them went to Arab countries talking to them to stop the support for the National Unity Government, especially the financial aid. They told them that if they stopped the financial aid that the National Unity Government would collapse by the end of the year and that that collapse would end the political programme of Hamas and so that would open the road for a new political peace process. For example [Rafir Husseini], he went to Brussels

---

11. This is Samir 'the hammer' el-Madhoun who, on Wednesday, 13 June, found himself surrounded in the Palestinian Presidential compound in Gaza by Hamas gunmen. Madhoun and several of his compatriots fought their way out of the compound after Madhoun taunted the Hamas platoon that had him surrounded: 'I will give you until three this afternoon to surrender,' he shouted. The next afternoon, stopped at a Hamas roadblock, he was recognized, mobbed by a pro-Hamas crowd and executed. Madhoun earned the nickname 'hammer' because he liked to execute Hamas officials by hitting them on the head with a hammer.
12. In Abu Mazen's house in Gaza.
13. Hamas officials have taken over the Interior Ministry buildings in Gaza, as well as the Presidential Compound and the headquarters of the Preventive Security Services. They have reported discovering files and computer discs of 'a highly sensitive nature'. There are five different categories of information, according to published reports: first, Preventive Security Service files of communications with American officials of an unspecified nature; second, Preventive Security Service intelligence leadership files on Hamas and other Palestinian leaders; third, lists of Hamas officials targeted for assassination; fourth, files on the personal lives of Palestinian officials and their wives and daughters that were intended to be used or that have been used for the purposes of blackmail; fifth, general US and Palestinian intelligence files of an unspecified nature dating back many years. An official in Abu Mazen's office noted: 'If these files are thorough, then Hamas will know just about every secret [that we have]. That means, the requests of foreign nations, funding, meetings, joint operations, you name it.'

and talked directly to the Europeans. I think you may have heard of this. Saeb Erekat did the same thing in the United States. When we faced Abu Mazen with these facts, saying we had some recorded things of this, he was angry. He said, 'I will not accept it. I will not accept it that this man is saying this or that. I am the man who expresses the official position of the President.' But it was clear that [Rafir Husseini] is his office manager and he was the one who sent him to the Europeans. He did not buy the ticket from Ramallah and go by himself, or on his own behalf. At the same time [Yasir Abed Rabbo] went and he said in public, in the United Arab Emirates, that supporting Hamas will damage the Palestinian cause.

So, we have come to this point. They are undermining the National Unity Government. They are supporting the siege against the Palestinian people. They are undermining the security plan and over that they are doing their best to damage the security in the territories in order to destroy everything. There was no other choice. We had no other choice. You have to make your own step against those people. So our step was very limited. We had to face those generals of the security forces who worked against the national benefits. Our actions were not against Fatah, they were not against the President, they were not against the security forces. We made that step and it was clear that no one of Fatah's leaders was attacked in Gaza – I'm talking about Gaza. Not one of their offices or their institutions was attacked. Even the security forces; we asked them to leave their offices before any attacks and if they did there were no attacks, there were no killings. For example in Rafah, you can check that, we took over all the offices without shooting anybody.

Michael Ancram: And the Marina?

Usamah Hamdan: The marina in Jubalya was the same. For example there were senior leaders from Fatah in Gaza, no one attacked them [Ahmed Hellas, Acre el Avaa, Sufran Abu Zaide] you have dozens of names. More than this, we called them. We knew there were some leaders in the security forces, they were involved in the killings; but we believe we want to solve our problem, we don't want to complicate the problem. If you guarantee their position we would release them, and that happened. With someone like [Misawa Hallerpersi], who was responsible for the massacre of Al Hidea Mosque, when about 30 people were killed in the mosque, I'm sorry to say this, in a way even the Israelis did not do that. It was not as it was done in Hebron [the Hebron Massacre of the early 1990s]. Rather, I am talking about an official security leader, an official security force, they did that in a mosque, killing more than 30 people and injuring more than 70 people.

Anyway, we said at this point that we have to talk clearly and frankly. The complications in the Palestinian situation resulted from the weakness of Abu Mazen. It resulted from the feeling that the United States and Israel may support, may generate a new leadership for the Palestinian people, which is Mohammad Dahlan. And it is the feeling that if Hamas could continue in power, forming the government, having the majority in the legislative council, this may not help the stability in the region. This wrong concept generated this result.

I believe we have to talk about the future. The first point: if you want to deal with the Palestinian people you have to deal with their elected leadership. If anyone thinks that he can generate a Palestinian leadership by financial support and by some political support he will complicate the situation and finally he will fail. And everyone noticed that in Gaza. They could not even survive for three days, even though they were supported by the international community, by the Israelis, for more than twelve years.

Second point: I believe, if you are talking about a solution, if you are talking about stability, you have to deal with a real committed movement, and it was clear in the last two years the most committed movement, for example, to the ceasefire was Hamas. It was not Fatah, it wasn't any other group.

The third point: I believe they can continue putting the Palestinian people under siege. But helping Abu Mazen by aid will not help him in front of his Palestinian people. Now – and we will say that in the future – he is a traitor. He is applying the outsider plans, he is doing the steps as the Israeli wants. This will not help him, this will not help his group.

So the solution is clear: to recognize the results of the elections. To respect the Palestinian democracy; to support the Palestinian people to secure the organizations; to secure their democratic systems, and to deal with them directly, talking about peace, security and the political process. This will lead us in the right direction. Otherwise, I believe the Palestinian people will defend their rights. They will defend their honour.

Michael Ancram: How do you get this new process started?

Usamah Hamdan: We have already started. In Gaza we call for the police to start their work. What had happened? General [Kamal Sheikh], who is the general command for the police, asked all the policemen in Gaza to return to their homes, not to do anything in the streets, and he will pay them their salaries and if anyone went to the street doing his job he will take him to a court martial. So it is clear that someone is trying to damage the whole situation while you are doing your best to apply the rule of the establishment, the institution. So the first point, we have a National Unity Government, and this National Unity Government is supposed to be supported.

There was a security plan endorsed by the government who are ready to start working on that. I believe we have to work in order to hold a national dialogue conference – all the groups are supposed to be invited – and then we can start our dialogue under the supervision of the Arabs – maybe some other people – but this time this dialogue is supposed to be supervised and there must be guarantees, anything which will be accepted. I mean the Palestinian people will agree it, it is supposed to be applied on the ground. If someone asked how to start the dialogue while there are problems on the ground? We did not say that we are taking over Gaza. We are asking the security forces to start their work back, and the ministers to start their work, they are working now but it is clear this security plan which was generated by [Dayton] and his colleagues will not work on the ground anymore.[14]

Michael Ancram: Has Saudi Arabia still got a role?

Usamah Hamdan: We have talked to Prince Saud al Faisal and we are still committed to the Mecca Agreement and he said that in the Arab League, and he said we believe we have to start from this agreement.[15] We appreciate this position and I think it will be a good point to start from. The Syrians support that, the Qatari, the Yemenis, Algeria, the Sudan, I think it's a good number of states that supported that. Even Amr Moussa he said on the phone that he accepts the idea – that was between him and Khaled Mashal.

Jonathan Lehrle: Is anybody seeing Amr Moussa in Beirut today? He comes in this evening.

Usamah Hamdan: He will come in today but [laughter] he probably has enough on his agenda, so this is probably not something that he will think about today.

Michael Ancram: At the moment if you look at the perception in the world you have a very strong propaganda operation on behalf of Abu Mazen, how do you counteract that?

Usamah Hamdan: They are repeating the same mistakes when they brought him for the first time as prime minister, when he came as a prime minister. By their propaganda they convinced all the Palestinian people that he was brought by them to be a prime minister, even Fatah people, they attacked him. When Abu Amar [Yasser Arafat] died and he became the president by their propaganda they showed that he is their man and this damaged him. Now they are damaging the remains of his reputation among the Palestinian people. When Condoleezza Rice talked to him on the phone telling him that she supports his steps, when President Bush talked to him telling him that he will lift the sanctions against a government that he had formed, when the support came directly from the European Union – this is damaging to all his reputation.

I believe Abu Mazen is losing his legitimacy inside the Palestinian community. And by their acts, by his people's acts on the ground … in the West Bank they attacked 150 institutions related to Hamas humanitarian – educational, clubs, support for sports, mosques, even libraries … so they attacked 150 institutions,

---

14. Usamah Hamdan and the Hamas leadership are here endorsing the security plan that resulted from the National Unity Government but which was not implemented.
15. As of 29 June, the Saudis have said publicly that they still retain their support for the National Unity Government. Their endorsement was followed by that of the head of the Arab League. Egypt and Jordan have endorsed the government of Abu Mazen. Syria has called for dialogue.

they burned them; I'm not saying attack, they damaged the doors, they burned them. They attacked the house of the Parliament Speaker, they burned it, even his family was in the house. They kidnapped 100 members of Hamas, they assassinated one of them, they attacked the elected municipalities. In Nablus they kicked them out and appointed a new municipality from Fatah, and they did that in [Beita] and [Safirt] and several municipalities. All that was done in just five days. And even they said that they have stopped this, up to today they are still attacking the people, destroying and damaging the national institutions.

This shows the people what is the meaning of security under their rule, what is the meaning of security by their security forces. It is not the al Aqsa brigades who are doing that. It is the Presidential guard, the Preventive Security Services and the intelligence services that are doing this.[16] I believe if this propaganda continues, if this support continues, this will not help Abu Mazen and it will not help the Palestinian situation.

Michael Ancram: Just so I'm clear. Your position is if you got back to the Mecca Agreement that would be the position. The conditions of Mecca, that would be a basis for restarting ... so Mecca is still the basis.

Usamah Hamdan: For us Mecca and the Cairo Agreement before that and the Palestinian National Conciliation Agreement which was agreed in June last year. It is still the basis and we are committed to the three of those agreements. I believe it was a temporary step in order to stop this, and to say, well, we have to apply what we have agreed on, and if there was international support for this I think we can have a new start in the Palestinian situation. And I believe after a while you can talk with a committed and a legitimate Palestinian leadership.

Michael Ancram: The reason I'm asking is that King Abdullah at the moment is in Spain, talking to the European leaders and he is taking the same view that Mecca must be the beginning. Yesterday we saw President Assad and he is of the same view. I had my foreign spokesman from my party with me and I told him the first message he must get back is that talking must begin again. At the moment if you look at the propaganda, the news, everybody is saying that Hamas is in Gaza so we must forget it and get on with the rest – that that is very dangerous.

Usamah Hamdan: They are claiming that we are killing and assassinating the people in Gaza. We said we are ready to have an Arab investigation committee in Gaza. They can come, they can stay, they can see everything on the ground. The one who rejected this is the other side, and I know why: they know what they have

---

16. The head of military and security intelligence in the West Bank is Tawfik Tarawi, formerly designated by the Israeli government as one of 'the Muqata terrorists'. Tarawi now maintains extensive files on Hamas, its networks in the West Bank, and its reach inside the religious community. His new headquarters, near the Presidential Compound, has – on its third floor – extensive files on each Hamas member and cell. Tarawi's operation is said to be supported by American funds.

done before, they know what they are doing now. I'm not saying that there were no mistakes this last few days. There were mistakes and it is clear we don't accept that and we will not let the people do these mistakes again. It is clear we are not defending the mistakes. We are not saying it did not happen. We have the courage to say this was wrong. The main problem is how to apply all the agreements. It is not accepted anymore to make those agreements in the first hours of the day but then not to apply them at the end of the day.

I'm not sure if you have this expression, they say – it is an Arabic expression – it means the talks in the night are done with butter, when the sun rises it will melt again. I'm not sure if you have something like this in English, but we will not accept this situation. If they really insist to reform the whole situation they have points from which to start from, the Mecca Agreement, Palestinian Conciliation and the Cairo Agreement from 2005. This time we will insist on supervision for this dialogue so everyone can know who is working positively and who is trying to damage the situation.

Michael Ancram: Who do you see doing the supervision?

Usamah Hamdan: As I said, we accept the Arab supervision and if there is anybody interested in that we will not say no for anyone.

Michael Ancram: And how difficult [will it be] for you to see the situation through? Abu Mazen is now given the money and Gaza is cut off.

Usamah Hamdan: There is an important point; we have to ask a big question. If the international community is interested in having Gaza separated from the West Bank, if they are, he can do that. If they are not, I think he will not do that. What will happen if they want this to happen? I believe this will give a chance for all the people who are against the democratic processes inside Palestine to say 'well you have tried, but it is not workable, so there is no real democracy'. And this will take us back to the position – there is no use to accept this system, there is no use to work with this system, the only solution is to burn up the system. Do you know what this will mean for the whole region? No one will accept the democracy anymore and this will minimize the space for the people who believe in democracy, the democrats, the political Islam. And this will widen the space for the people who talking about burning the system. I believe this will not secure the region.

Mark Perry: If he (Abu Mazen) agrees to the separation of the West Bank and Gaza, he has crossed the red line.

Usamah Hamdan: That's right.

Mark Perry: Because no Palestinian could ever agree to the separation of the West Bank and Gaza, just as no Palestinian could ever agree to give up the Right of Return.

Usamah Hamdan: That's right, but if somebody was supposing to cross that line, I believe he will lose everything as a Palestinian leadership. No one will respect him as a leader, because the Palestinian people insist for all time on having a united nation. They are still talking about the refugees outside the Palestinian territories, they are still talking about the people inside Israel as Palestinians. If you ask anyone, he will not accept the idea of being an Israeli, an Arab-Israeli, he will tell you directly he is a Palestinian. So if he crosses that line, I think he will lose it.

Michael Ancram: Very interesting. It has been helpful for me because I'm going back on Thursday and would be able to give some counter-information.

Usamah Hamdan: I will try to follow-up today and tomorrow to see if we have some contacts with the Saudis and others, if there is anything new I will try to let you know.

Mark Perry: How is the Central Committee with Abu Mazen's decision?

Usamah Hamdan: There are some people who are not accepting that. Abbas Zaki told me frankly that he is basically against that, and I was shocked by that. He told me. But he is a weak man, you cannot count on him, he may change his position from this chair to that chair. And I believe he is corrupted. Two million is not a little piece of money.

Mark Perry: What about the others?

Usamah Hamdan: Hani al-Hassan, he said clearly that this will damage everything.[17] But Hani['s position] is weak. Farouk Quddumi, he said nothing, he called for keeping the unity of Fatah.

Mark Perry: Where is Dahlan?

Usamah Hamdan: He is in Ramallah, he was in Egypt, he was in Taba.

Mark Perry: I understand that there was a telephone call in which a colleague of Abu Mazen's said that Abu Mazen said that he wished that Dahlan would stay in Egypt. And this colleague said that Abu Mazen said he hoped that Dahlan had been humbled and that maybe all that would happen is that Salam Fayad would resign but the government would stay intact. The plan, I had heard, was for Dahlan to stay in Egypt, but when I woke up next morning to hear that Abu Mazen had

---

17. On 27 June, senior Fatah leader, Hani al-Hassan, spoke out in an interview on the pan-Arab TV network, al Jazeera, where, *Al-Ahram Weekly* reports, 'he argued that the recent showdown in Gaza was not a confrontation between Fatah and Hamas but one between Hamas and the Dahlan faction ... Following the interview, representatives of the Dahlan faction called Abbas, pressuring him to fire and punish Al-Hassan, while masked gunmen opened fire on his home in Ramallah. Al-Hassan was not in Ramallah during the attack.'

dissolved the government and that Dahlan was in Ramallah, I assume the Americans put him there?

Usamah Hamdan: That's right. Abu Mazen has problems. His main problem is that he is a weak man, that he can't make decisions and he is under pressure now but that does not mean he is not responsible. He has some responsibility but he is not acting as a president. They prevented him coming to Gaza four days before the clashes. He talked to Ismail Haniya on the phone and said he told him I am coming and will not leave before solving the problem. Then two days later…

Mark Perry: Usamah, all he has going for him is the internal security service and the Presidential Guard and Mohammad Dahlan. He doesn't have the rest of them.

Usamah Hamdan: That's right.

Mark Perry: At the end of the day Abu Ala is broken.

Michael Ancram: What if he has money to hand out?

Mark Perry: You know what, the Americans will not deliver. Any money will go astray, into condominiums, that money will not reach where it is supposed to.

Michael Ancram: You mentioned, it is a small thing but could be quite important in Britain. You mentioned that Alan Johnston's captors were a family…

Usamah Hamdan: The Dagmoush family.

Michael Ancram: That they were associated with Dahlan. Would Dahlan have known?

Usamah Hamdan: Yes. He knew this, he does. And three times we came to the point to release Alan Johnston and by telephone call from [Samir Musharawi], who is Dahlan's man, they stopped that.

Jonathan Lehrle: And what about now, because Hamas gave a deadline?

Usamah Hamdan: Well now, in one point which we are working on is to have the man secure and safe. If you did anything wrong they may hurt him, so we are making the pressure slowly in order to have him released. We are talking to some senior members of the family, telling them this will not help the whole family, and they have to play a role, they can't cover their backs while they are kidnapping this man.[18]

---

18. BBC reporter Alan Johnston was released by the Army of Islam on 4 July 2007.

Jonathan Lehrle: And the response from them, they understand, they are listening to this seriously?

Usamah Hamdan: Yes, well I believe so. It is dangerous, so can't make a militant attack against them, but you have to pressure them slowly, slowly in order to have this man released. The most important thing is that our people know him well (Alan Johnston), they know him well. I've talked yesterday to our [person there in Gaza]. He saw him dozens of times, not in public, he visited him in his office. They respect him. They believe they have to do the job slowly in order not to hurt him.

Printed here with grateful acknowledgements to Conflicts Forum (www.conflictsforum.org)

Usamah Hamdan is a senior member of the Islamic Resistance Movement and is the Hamas Representative in Lebanon.

Michael Ancram is a United Kingdom Conservative Party politician and Member of Parliament for Devizes. In May 1993, he was appointed Parliamentary Under-Secretary of State at the Northern Ireland Office. In January 1994, he was appointed Minister of State at the Northern Ireland Office. In September 2001, he was appointed Deputy Leader of the Opposition and Shadow Secretary of State for Foreign & Commonwealth Affairs; in November 2003, he also become Shadow Secretary of State for International Affairs. Until December 2005, he was Shadow Secretary of State for Defence and Deputy Leader of the Party. He has been a regular interlocutor with Hamas and Hezbollah officials as a guest of Conflicts Forum in Beirut.

Jonathan Lehrle is the Director of the London-based Global Strategy Forum, an independent think-tank which researches and stimulates discussion on international and security issues largely, but not exclusively, from the standpoint of the UK national interest. In 2001 he was appointed Chief of Staff to the Shadow Foreign Secretary and Deputy Leader, Michael Ancram QC MP, a position he held until December 2005. The transcript of this interview was provided by Jonathan Lehrle.

Mark Perry is an American author and historian and Co-Director of Conflicts Forum, an international organization that seeks an opening to political Islam.

Israel

Mythologizing a twentieth century accident

Gabriel Kolko

One of the many quirks of the nineteenth century's intellectual heritage was the great intensification of nationalism and – to quote one expert – the creation of 'nation-ness', the consequences of which have varied dramatically all the way from the negligible to the crucial (as in the case of Israel) to war and peace in a vast strategic region. There was, of course, often a basis for various nationalisms to build upon, but the essentially artificial function of forming nations from very little or nothing was common.

Wars were the most conducive to this enterprise, and the emergence of what was termed socialism after 1914 – which had a crucial nationalist basis in such places as China and Vietnam – was due to the fact that foreign invasions greatly magnified nationalism's ability to build on ephemeral foundations to merge socialism and patriotism. For a vital component of nationalism, often its sole one, was a hatred of foreigners – 'others' – giving it largely a negative function rather than an assertion of distinctive values and traits essential to a unique entity. Myths, often far-fetched and irrational, were built. Zionism is the focus of this discussion but it was scarcely alone.[1]

Vienna was surely the most intellectually creative place in the world at the end of the nineteenth century. Economics, art, philosophy, political theories on the Right as well as Left, psychoanalysis – Vienna gave birth or influenced most of them. Ideas had to be very original to be noticed, and most were. We must understand the unique and rare innovative environment in which Theodore Herzl, an assimilated Hungarian Jew who became the founder of Zionism, functioned. For a time he was also a German nationalist, and went through phases admiring Richard Wagner and Martin Luther. Herzl was many things, including a very efficient organizer, but he was also very conservative and feared that Jews without a state – especially those in Russia – would become revolutionaries.

A state based on religion rather than the will

Gabriel Kolko's recent books include The Age of War *(Lynne Rienner Publishers), an extract from which was featured in* Spokesman 91.

of all of its inhabitants was at the end of the nineteenth century not only a medieval notion but also a very eccentric idea, one Herzl concocted in the rarified environment of cafés where ideas were produced with scant regard for reality. It was also full of countless contradictions, based not merely on the conflicts between theological dogmas and democracy but also vast cultural differences among Jews, all of which were to appear later. Europe's Jews have precious little in common, and their mores and languages are very distinct. But the gap between Jews from Europe and those from the Arab world was far, far greater. Moreover, there were many radically different kinds of Zionism within a small movement, ranging from the religiously motivated to Marxists who wanted to cease being Jews altogether and, as Ber Borochov would have it, become 'normal'. In the end, all that was to unite Israel was a military ethic premised on a hatred of those 'others' around them – and it was to become a warrior-state, a virtual Sparta dominated by its army. Initially, at least, Herzl had the fate of Russian and East European Jews in mind; the outcome was very different.

Zionism was original but at the turn of the century its following was close to non-existent. An important exception was the interest of Lord Rothschild. Moreover, from its inception Zionism was symbiotic on Great Powers – principally Great Britain – that saw it as a way of spreading their colonial ambitions to the Middle East. As early as 1902 Herzl met with Joseph Chamberlain, then British Colonial Secretary, to further Zionist claims in the region bordering Egypt, and the following year he hired David Lloyd George – later to become prime minister – to handle the Zionist case.[2] Herzl also unsuccessfully asked the sultan of the Ottoman Empire if he might obtain Palestine, after which he advocated establishing a state in Uganda – although his followers much preferred the Holy Land. Only the principle of a Jewish State, anywhere, appealed to him – but mainly for Jews in the Russian Empire. Herzl was only the first in the Zionist tradition of advocating a state for others; he was never in favour of all Jews moving there. Chaim Weizmann wrote to Herzl in 1903 that the large majority of the young Jews in Russia were anti-Zionist because they were revolutionaries – which only reinforced Herzl's convictions. In 1913, British Intelligence estimated that perhaps one per cent of the Jews had Zionist affiliations, a figure that rose in the Russian Pale – which contained about six million Jews – as the war became longer.

It was scarcely an accident that, in November 1917, Lord Arthur Balfour was to make Britain's historic endorsement of a Jewish homeland in their newly mandated territory of Palestine in a letter to Rothschild. Some of these Englishmen also shared the Biblical view that it was the destiny of Jews to return to their ancient soil. Others thought that this gesture would help keep Russia in the war, and that nefarious Jews had the influence to do so. Most saw a Jewish state as a means of consolidating British power in the vast Islamic region.[3]

Jewish migration: many promised lands

Migration has been one of the universal phenomena of world history since time immemorial, and we know a great deal about its causes and motives. People migrate mainly out of necessity, generally economic, and they choose from existing options. They very rarely go someplace for the 'blessings of liberty', or ideology; if they do, such variable factors as economic deprivation or changes in laws should not exist. But in the case of Palestine and Zionism, Jews behaved like people everywhere and at most times.

It is a Zionist myth that there were many Jews who wished to go to a primitive, hot, dusty place and did so. They did not – and all of the available numbers prove this conclusively. After the Bolshevik Revolution of October 1917, the Pale was abolished and a very large number of the Jews in it moved to Russia's cities; many of them saw the Bolsheviks as liberators and filled the ranks of the revolution at every level.[4] If they emigrated, and here the numbers are very important, it was not – if they had a choice – to Palestine.

From 1890 to 1924, about two million of the 20 million immigrants to the United States were Jews – overwhelmingly from Eastern Europe. Other nations in the Western Hemisphere also attracted about a million Jews during this period, to which we must add Jewish migration to South Africa, Australia, Western Europe, and the like. This does not mean that Jews were not 'Zionists', but they had no intention whatsoever of embarking on *Aliyah* – of going to Palestine themselves. As Herzl believed, it was a project for others.

Jews in the Diaspora, like most ethnic groups, banded together in numerous organizations and nostalgia – and confusion – soon overwhelmed them. Organized Zionism grew in the United States, as it had not in Eastern Europe – but it demanded only money, thereby ultimately making Israel viable.

In 1893, there were an estimated 10,000 Jews in Palestine, 61,000 in 1920, and 122,000 in 1925. All of these figures are only the best-informed estimates; there were censuses in 1922 and 1931 only, and even the 1922 numbers are contested. But the general trend is beyond doubt and very clear. For every Jew who went to Palestine from 1890 to 1924, at least 27 went to the Western Hemisphere alone. Relatively, the Zionist project was the utopian dream of a tiny minority and it would have failed save for two factors: the Holocaust, and the much-overlooked fact that, in 1924, the United States passed a new immigration law based on quotas using the nationalities distribution in the 1890 census as a basis, effectively cutting off migration from Eastern and Southern Europe to a mere trickle of what it had been.

In 1924, Jewish population in Palestine increased 5.9 per cent, but in 1925 – the first year the American law went into effect – it leaped 28 per cent, and 23 per cent in 1926. This was still a small minority of the Jews who left Europe, but this sudden spurt was directly related to American policy. From 1927 to 1932 it never grew more than 5.3 per cent annually and, in 1927, it was a mere 0.2 per cent.[5] Very few Jews went to Palestine, and a small proportion of them were ideologically motivated; the vast majority migrated elsewhere.

The British had always been in favour of Jewish migration and, after 1933, it grew greatly – Jews were six per cent of the Palestinian population in 1912 but 29 percent in 1935 – but now it was increasingly composed of Jews from Germany rather than Poland. These Jews had to get out of Germany, where the Zionist movement had always been very weak, and they were scarcely ideological zealots. Had there been open migration to the United States they would have gone there. Arab riots after 1935 compelled the British to reduce the inflow and, in 1939, they adopted a White Paper enforcing strict restrictions on immigration.

What is certain is that Hitler's importance must always be set in a larger context. Without him there never would have been a flow of Jews out of Germany, and very probably no state of Israel, but also crucial was the US 1924 Immigration Act. Migrants went to Palestine out of necessity, in the vast majority of cases, not choice. Both of these factors were crucial, and to determine their relative importance is an abstract, futile enterprise. But without either, the Zionist project of creating a Jewish state in Palestine would have remained another exotic Viennese concoction, never to be realized, because while the Jews in the Diaspora were in favour of a Jewish state, virtually none living in safe nations were ever to uproot themselves and embark on *Aliyah* – the return to the ancient homeland. They had no reason to do so.

There were many promised lands and Herzl's exotic ruminations were scarcely the inspiration for the flow of Jews out of Europe. Israel's existence was an unpredictable accident of history. The past century has been full of them, everywhere. That is why the world is in such a perilous condition.

References
1. Benedict Anderson, *Imagined Communities: Reflections on the Origin and Spread of Nationalism*, London, Verso, 1983, pp. 4-6.
2. David Fromkin, *A Peace to End All Peace: The Fall of the Ottoman Empire and the Creation of the Modern Middle East*, New York, Henry Holt, 1989, pp. 272-3, 278, 317.
3. William M. Johnston, *The Austrian Mind: An Intellectual and Social History, 1848-1938,* Berkeley, University of California Press, 1972, pp. 357-61; Yuri Slezkine, *The Jewish Century*, Princeton University Press, 2004, pp. 149-52; David Fromkin, *A Peace to End All Peace, op. cit.,* pp. 272, 294.
4. Yuri Slezkine, *The Jewish Century, passim.*
5. Data on Palestine is from *Population of Ottoman and Mandate Palestine: Statistical and Demographic Considerations*, 2002-05, pp. 5, 6, 11 and *passim*. http://www.mideastweb.org/palpop.htm

The man without a country

James Alexander Thom

A 'phone and pen pal' of Kurt Vonnegut's, James Alexander Thom sent us this tribute.

When Kurt Vonnegut died in April, he left an almost palpable 'wisdom vacuum' here in America, so much so that I found it hard to breathe.

There hadn't been much wisdom in evidence since the turn of the century anyway. We'd hear all about 'data' and 'intelligence', but 'wisdom' had become an archaic word. (As we soon learned, the data and intelligence weren't all that great, either.) But when the United States suffered a stupidity epidemic and let George W. Bush start an unprovoked war, old Kurt Vonnegut brought his pen out of retirement and pitted it against Bush's sword.

His final book, *A Man Without a Country*, became a bestseller and heartened us with its sad, funny, kindly wisdom. It is a part of America's awakening from war fever. Vonnegut, who had been through war, is a world authority on peace, and a beloved national wise man. He dwarfs Bush, who has never had a shred of combat experience or wisdom, and apparently thinks peace is just too boring.

One of the wisest things Kurt Vonnegut did over the years was to keep reminding us of what earlier wise men said. You could tell whom he admired by the opportunities he took to quote them. Jesus, Abraham Lincoln, Mark Twain and Eugene Debs, to put them in chronological order. He quoted their wisdom in favour of human kindness and justice and against war-making.

Three of the best evenings I ever had in public involved Mr Vonnegut, who was, like me, Indiana-born. In the early 1990s we dined together at a big table during a literary festival in Indianapolis, as guest novelists. He was warm, droll and charming as usual, but tended to steer the conversation towards suicide (which he'd once failed to accomplish).

It seems he was having sympathetic angst for his friend and peer, William Styron, who had been struggling with suicidal depression. I had the pleasure of watching and hearing my

Shawnee Indian wife scold the great man for even considering such a thing. She had never met Kurt before that evening, but had perceived that he was too valuable an American treasure to deliberately deprive us of his own life. By the time dinner was over, he was off that dismal subject and twinkling with good humour. Either she had convinced him, or made him afraid to be scolded about it again by an outspoken Shawnee woman. Whatever it was, he soldiered on for another fifteen years or so. I like to believe she made a bit of a difference.

The second great evening was also in Indianapolis, about ten years later, when he was scheduled to speak to the Indiana Civil Liberties Union, but wasn't well enough to come out from New York. I was asked to substitute for him.

I had no idea what he'd planned to say, but that was in the days when John Ashcroft was making a pious, unconstitutional ass of himself as George Bush's first Attorney General, so I had plenty to say. (Bush sure can pick those A.G.s!) When Kurt read my speech later, he phoned to tell me it was better than what he could have done – which was very kind, but surely not true.

The wonderful thing about that evening for me was the feeling in the auditorium that, even though I wasn't the man they'd signed up to hear, we all felt that we were sharing in the defence of American Constitutional law against a gang of delusionary rogues who had seized the White House by *coup d'état*, and we were declaring ourselves defenders of the Constitution.

And, as Kurt would have done, I had used humour as our defensive weapon. We were comrades-in-arms with mirth on our faces.

My last good Vonnegut evening was here in Bloomington, Indiana, in 2006, where I was invited to recite some of his anti-war words as one of the readers in Anthony Arnove's 'Voices of a People's History' stage production, based on Howard Zinn's classic history book. The selection began with a question I had asked myself, and Kurt had written, a question about wisdom: 'Where are Abraham Lincoln and Mark Twain now when we need them?' I couldn't have imagined a happier combination: Twain, my favourite dead American author. Vonnegut, my favourite (then) living one. Lincoln, the greatest writer who was ever President of the United States, or maybe any country. Zinn, my favourite historian.

I had just finished writing a novel, 'Saint Patrick's Battalion', about the US-Mexico War of 1846-48, which was started by President James Polk almost the same way Bush started the Iraq War. Kurt had encouraged me to write the novel because it was so timely. And I had dedicated the book to him.

In the Vonnegut script selected for me to read that night was a quotation from Abraham Lincoln, who as a young Congressman had objected to that invasion. Here was Lincoln's stunningly written indictment of Polk (which now fits Bush exactly):

> 'Trusting to escape scrutiny, by fixing the public gaze upon the exceeding brightness of military glory – that attractive rainbow that rises in showers of blood ... he plunged into war.'

The last reader that evening dramatized the words of famous anti-war mother Cindy Sheehan in a hair-raising delivery, and if Bush the warmonger had wandered into that auditorium that evening, his Secret Service bodyguards would have had all they could do to shield him from the contempt of that crowd of peacemongers.

Kurt Vonnegut used his own words to prove the pen is mightier than the sword, but also he enthusiastically relayed the anti-war writings of others. When I wrote how an old ex-Marine feels about the massacre of Iraqi civilians by young Marines in the town of Haditha, Kurt urged me to send the piece to this publication (*The Spokesman no.92*), where it appeared last year.

I thanked him for helping me spread my anti-war words, and for letting me spread his.

'I'm a man of peace', that old WWII rifleman and secular humanist said to me on the phone. 'God bless you.'

Those were the last words I ever heard from him in his own voice, and if they weren't nice, I don't know what is.

Fighting for Trade Union freedom

Build peace not bombs - no new Trident

Bob Crow
General Secretary

John Leach
President

Kurt is up in Heaven now

Kurt Vonnegut

The death of Kurt Vonnegut was a great blow to The Spokesman. *In 2003, Kurt was invited to speak under the auspices of the Mark Twain House in Hartford, Connecticut '...at the age of eighty, and because of what I myself have written'. He sent us the text, which we published as a pamphlet* (Spokesman Books £2). *We thought it would be appropriate to reprint it here as a tribute to our friend.*

Hello. Ahoy. I hope this isn't like the Academy Awards, where nobody was supposed to say what the great American patriot and moralist, Mark Twain, would have said at this crisis in our history, upon receiving a Lifetime Achievement Award, say.

Michael Moore in fact violated that standard of decorum at the Academy Awards. Shame on Michael Moore. He spoiled the party.

First things first: I want it clearly understood that this mustache I'm wearing is my father's mustache. I should have brought his photograph. My big brother Bernie, now dead, a physical chemist who discovered that silver iodide can sometimes make it snow or rain – he wore it, too.

Speaking of weather: Mark Twain said some readers complained that there wasn't enough weather in his stories. So he wrote some weather, which they could insert wherever they thought it would help some.

Mark Twain, and I forget what his real name was – Justin Kaplan, the great Twain scholar, is among us tonight. He will know what Mark Twain's name really was. So ask him.

In any case, the person who called himself Mark Twain was said to have shed a tear of gratitude and incredulousness when honored for his writing by Oxford University in England. And I should shed a tear, surely, having been asked at the age of eighty, and because of what I myself have written, to speak under the auspices of the sacred Mark Twain House here in Hartford.

What other American landmark is as sacred to me as the Mark Twain House? The Lincoln Memorial in Washington, DC. Mark Twain and Abraham Lincoln were country boys from Middle America, and both of them made the American people laugh at themselves and appreciate really important, really moral jokes.

Abraham Lincoln was 26 years older than Twain. Queen Victoria was only 16 years older than Twain, and so might have been his sister. Twain and Victoria died in the same decade. Victoria in 1901 and Twain in 1910.

And I do not kid myself. Aside from my mustache and my addiction to nicotine, I stand in relationship to Mark Twain as Antonio Salieri stood to Wolfgang Amadeus Mozart.

I should tell you, too, that tonight I will occasionally mention somebody named 'Jim.' Jim is the most appealing and wise character in the greatest possible of all American novels. In company such as this, I do not need to say the name of that book. It's not 'Gone with the Wind.'

I note that construction has stopped here in Hartford of a Mark Twain Museum – behind the carriage house of the Mark Twain House at 351 Farmington Avenue.

Work persons have been sent home from that site because American 'Conservatives,' as they call themselves, on Wall Street and at the head of so many of our corporations, have stolen a major fraction of our private savings, have ruined investors and employees by means of fraud and outright piracy.

Shock and awe.

And now, having installed themselves as our Federal Government, or taken control of it from outside, they have squandered our public treasury and then some. They have created a public debt of such appalling magnitude that our descendents, for whom we had such high hopes, will come into this world as poor as churchmice.

And our nation and our states, cities and towns, and so many of our people are dead broke, or close to it on account of 9/11?

You know what I say about that? I say, 'horsefeathers.'

And if you think Baghdad is a mess tonight, wait until you see New York and Chicago and Denver and Los Angeles two or three years from now, not because of Arabs, whom TV is teaching our children to hate, but because of what home grown economic terrorists have done to them.

Shock and awe.

What are the Conservatives doing with all the money and power which used to belong to all of us? They are telling us to be absolutely terrified, and to run round in circles like chickens with their heads cut off. But they will save us. They are making us take off our shoes at airports. Can anybody here think of a more hilarious practical joke than that one?

Smile, America. You're on Candid Camera.

And they have turned loose a myriad of our high tech weapons, each one costing more than a hundred high schools, on a Third World country, in order to shock and awe human beings like us, like Jim, like Adam and Eve, between the Tigris and Euphrates Rivers.

In high school in Indianapolis I learned to call that part of the world 'The Cradle of Civilization.'

'Cradle?' Rock-a-bye baby.

And, oh yes, they're buying or building mansions in Palm Beach, Florida, and so on, in order to live like and near Rush Limbaugh. Some of them, I guess, are now driving Hummers instead of Beamers.

The other day I asked the former Yankees pitcher Jim Bouton what he thought of our great victory over Iraq, and he said, 'Mohammed Ali *versus* Mr. Rogers.' I assume that all of you, like Jim Bouton, a very funny writer by the way, watch 'Sesame Street.'

'Mohammed Ali *versus* Mr Rogers.'

What are Conservatives? They are people who will move Heaven and Earth, if they have to, who will ruin a company or a country or a planet, to prove to us and themselves that they are superior to everybody else, except for pals. They take good care of their pals, keep them out of jail – and so on.

Conservatives are crazy as bedbugs. They are bullies. Shock and awe.

Class war? You bet.

They have proved their superiority to admirers of Abraham Lincoln and Mark Twain and Jesus of Nazareth by, with an able assist from television, making inconsequential our protests against their war. On what grounds did we protest it? There are many I could name, but I need name only one, which is common sense.

I asked a Civil War historian one time what it was that poor whites in the Confederacy, who had never owned slaves, thought they had to fight so hard for. And he said it was so there could continue to be a great number of human beings who were mistreated legally and socially as their inferiors.

Even though they weren't billionaires, they were still Conservatives.

Were these Johnny Rebs scientifically correct in believing themselves mentally superior to the slaves? I'll have to say, 'Not quite.'

Some people similar in appearance to the character Jim in 'Huckleberry Finn,' but surely not all of them, have since performed superbly in all arts and sciences, and in all professions.

Some Jims, moreover, have given a gift to the world which is now almost the only reason many foreigners still like us at least a little bit. That gift is a specific remedy for the world-wide epidemic of depression, which is jazz, and in particular the Blues.

Albert Murray, a person of colour who is a friend of mine, is a jazz historian. He told me that the suicide rate per capita of slave owners was higher than that of slaves. He said that was because the slaves could do what white people only later learned how to do, which was to shoo away Old Man Suicide by playing and singing the Blues.

If I may insert an autobiographical note at this point: When I was growing up in Indianapolis during the Great Depression, the sanest, wisest, calmest person in our house was our cook Ida Young.

> If somebody says, 'It ain't the money,' it's the money.
> If a Conservative says, 'It ain't racism,' it's racism.
> If a Conservative says, 'It ain't xenophobia,' it's xenophobia.
> Shock and awe.

Foreigners loves us for our jazz. And they don't hate us for our purported liberty and justice for all. They hate us now for our arrogance. But they have hated us in the past because our corporations have long been the principal deliverers and imposers of new technologies and economic schemes which have wrecked the self-respect, the cultures of men, women and children in so many other countries.

Be that as it may, construction of the Mark Twain Museum will sooner or later be resumed. And I, the son and grandson of Indiana architects, seize this opportunity to suggest two features which I hope will be included in the completed structure. One is words to be chiseled into the capstone over the main entrance.

I would also like there to be a statue somewhere on the property, possibly one as tall as a giant redwood, considering the importance of the subject. Such a statue, even if only six feet high, would make an unfulfilled dream of Mark Twain's come true at last, at last. He found it unbearable, or so he said, that nowhere on Earth was there a monument to the most important human being who ever lived, who was Adam. He thought that Elmira, New York, where he was living then, would be a good place to put one at public expense.

What did Adam look like? Well, on that score at least you are in luck tonight. It so happens that I hold a Master's Degree in Anthropology from the University of Chicago. And by the power thus vested in me, I tell you that the fossil record now makes it incontrovertible that all of us, like the character Jim in 'Huckleberry Finn,' come from Africa.

Twain himself confessed to a shortage of weather in what he wrote. Modern readers surely note another shortfall, something else which is singularly missing. I mean erotica in its narrowest sense. I mean sex.

The same charge, of course, can be leveled against the collected works of Ralph Waldo Emerson and Henry David Thoreau.

The sexiest thing our hero ever wrote, I think, is 'Eve's Diary.' Talk about hard-core porn!

I would be delighted if one of you would contradict me.

Anyone? Justin Kaplan?

If we accept 'erotica' in its broader sense, as not just about sex between people, but about love affairs with anything, even ladies' shoes or crack cocaine or E-mail or coathangers, we can say Mark Twain wrote an erotic masterpiece which, in intensity of intercourse, makes 'Lady Chatterley's Lover' read like an op ed piece in the *New York Times*.

It is also the happiest book ever written.

I am speaking, of course, of 'Life on the Mississippi.'

The love object in that case of '*pyschopathia sexualis*', if you like, is a river.

Herman Melville, author of the second greatest possible American novel, was in love with the ocean.

I myself grew up in Indianapolis, the world's largest city not on a navigable waterway. I had only a race track and the Eli Lilly Company to fall in love with, and it shows. It shows.

On the subject of sexual perversions, I am dying to tell a joke which unfortunately involves the Irish. And the last thing I want to do, God knows, is to insult a person of Irish descent. I am nearly as indebted to the Irishpersons George Bernard Shaw and Oscar Wilde and Jonathan Swift as I am to Mark Twain and Herman Melville.

And, oh yes, I know Swift's parents were English. But he was born in Dublin, and that is where he received his education, which was evidently a good one. And you know what the Englishman Samuel Johnson said about 'Gulliver's Travels?' He said, 'Once you thought of the little people, the rest was obvious.'

But OK, here goes: You know what the definition of an Irish homosexual is? That's a man who loves women more than whiskey. I will pause, in order to let that sink in.

'A man who loves women more than *whiskey*.'

A violation of the natural order.

OK? So now, on that model, and it's a tricky one, I offer a definition of a homosexual male novelist in Victorian times. That was a man who loved women more than boats.

Most of you here though, because you have chosen to be in this place tonight, male or female, rich or poor, in your American dreams have lived on the beach or bank of a perfectly tremendous idea, and I quote:

> 'Fourscore and seven years ago our fathers brought forth on this continent, a new nation, conceived in Liberty, and dedicated to the proposition that all men are created equal.'

What a beckoning river or ocean that dream of equality has been for some!

The man who said that was shot to death in the back of his head by a young Conservative. John Wilkes Booth was only twenty-seven years old when he so exercised his rights under the Second Amendment to the Constitution. Twain was thirty.

Hello, Charlton Heston. You know what the Second Amendment actually says, if read in full? It says, 'Hey, Charlton Heston, please protect us. Join the National Guard.'

When our political ancestors said, eleven score and seven years ago now, that we were going to respect one another as equals, they were, except for Benjamin Franklin, who wanted to outlaw slavery, windbags. I am not telling you the news. We all know that.

But the Mark Twain House here in Hartford and the Lincoln Memorial in Washington celebrate two of our spiritual ancestors who wished with all their hearts and minds that the United States could really be a country of respected equals, or at least more of one.

Many of us, but obviously not all Americans, at this, the start of the Third Christian Millennium, wish that the whole Earth could be more of a home of respected equals. But our nation, and hence our whole planet, has been captured by Jingos and Yahoos and Know-nothings and bullying anti-equality Imperialists of a sort which so humiliated and sickened Twain and Lincoln in their day.

Should we give up? I hate to tell you, but our hero Mark Twain gave up on the whole human race in 1898. He was only sixty-three. He had twelve more years to live, and there hadn't even been a First World War yet. He wouldn't live long enough to hear about the First World War.

But, even so, he wrote 'The Mysterious Stranger.' In that tale, which would only be published posthumously, he suggests to his own grim satisfaction, and to mine as well, that Satan rather than God may have created this World, and, and I quote, 'The damned human race.'

So we could be demons in Hell. That would certainly explain a lot.

Was Twain a prophet? Technically, I guess we would have to say so. He said that, given human nature, things can only get worse. And things have gotten worse. Bingo.

At the end of 'A Connecticut Yankee in King Arthur's Court,' with knights being cooked to death in their iron suits when they tried to scale a fence charged with high voltage Yankee electricity, Twain foresaw how technology was going to revolutionize for the worse the manly arts of warfare. Bingo.

I myself have written that our planet's immune system is trying to get rid of a disease called 'us.' That would explain AIDS and the new pneumonia and driving while drunk and so on. And war.

But hey, listen:

I got a letter from a sappy woman a while back. She knew I was sappy, too, a fan of Twain and Lincoln – and Thoreau and George Bernard Shaw. She was about to have a baby. It wasn't mine. She just wanted to know if it was bad to bring such a sweet, innocent creature into a world as nasty as this one is.

I replied that what made being alive almost worthwhile for me was the saints I met, and they were numerous, and could be anywhere. These were Americans who behaved helpfully, capably, compassionately, honorably and modestly, in what might indeed be Hell.

I told her not to get an abortion, because there would be plenty of saints for her child to meet.

It was with such saints in mind that I came up with my first idea, since discarded, for a greeting to be chiseled into the capstone over the entrance to the Mark Twain Museum. This was it:

WELCOME TO UNDAMNED MEMBERS
OF THE HUMAN RACE.

But here is what I now think would be more fun to put up there, and Mark Twain loved fun more than anything. I have tinkered again with something famous he said, which is: 'Be good and you will be lonesome.' That is from 'Following the Equator.' OK?

So envision what a majestic front entrance the Mark Twain Museum will have someday. And imagine that these words have been chiseled into the noble capstone and painted gold:

BE GOOD AND YOU WILL BE LONESOME
MOST PLACES,
BUT NOT HERE, NOT HERE.

Another possible definition of an American saint: A person who does his or her job competently, without wanting to humble anyone, without wanting to make anybody who is economically or politically or socially weak feel like something the cat drug in.

And so much for American domestic policy. Now about American foreign policy:

One of the most humiliated and heartbroken pieces Twain ever wrote was about the slaughter of one hundred Moro men, women and children by our soldiers during our liberation of the people of the Philippines after the Spanish American War. Our brave commander was Leonard Wood, who now has a fort named after him. Fort Leonard Wood.

What did Abraham Lincoln have to say about such American imperialist wars? Those are wars which, on one noble pretext or another, actually aim to increase the natural resources and pools of tame labor available to the richest Americans who have the best political connections.

And it is almost always a mistake to mention Abraham Lincoln in a speech about something or somebody else. I am about to quote him again. He always steals the show. I guess he's already stolen this one.

I owe my awareness of the quotation to Morley Safer of Sixty Minutes, whose wife Jane, an anthropologist like me, comes from Hartford. Small world.

Morley Safer used this quotation in a speech and knocked my block off. Now I will use it in a speech and knock your blocks off. I see no reason why any of you shouldn't subsequently use it in speeches, in order to knock other people's blocks off.

Lincoln was only a Congressman when he said in 1848 what I am about to echo. He was heartbroken and humiliated by our war on Mexico, which had never attacked us.

We were making California our own, and a lot of other people and properties, and doing it as though butchering Mexican soldiers who were only defending their homeland against invaders weren't murder.

What other stuff besides California? Well, Texas, New Mexico, Utah, Nevada, Arizona, and parts of Colorado and Wyoming. Lots of ski resorts! I am not a racist, God knows, God knows, but one can't help wondering what a Mexican would want with a ski resort. A golf course, yes. But a ski resort?

The person Congressman Lincoln had in mind when he said what he said was James Polk, our President at the time. Abraham Lincoln said of Polk, his President, our armed forces' Commander and Chief:

> 'Trusting to escape scrutiny by fixing the public gaze upon the exceeding brightness of military glory, that attractive rainbow that rises in showers of blood – that serpent's eye, that charms to destroy, he plunged into war.'

Holy smokes! I almost said, 'Holy shit!' And I thought I was a writer! Twain was only 13 when Lincoln so wrote.

I asked Morley Safer where in heck he found that quotation, that 'rainbow of military glory rising in showers of blood,' and he said it was in a collection of Lincoln's letters in a library.

It wasn't in Bartlett's *Familiar Quotations*, but it will be in the next edition. What makes me think so? It so happens that Justin Kaplan, whom I have identified in our midst as our greatest Twain scholar, is also editor of that useful volume, that ticket to immortality.

Do you know we actually captured Mexico City during the Mexican War? Why isn't that a national holiday? And why isn't the face of James Polk up on Mount Rushmore, along with Ronald Reagan's?

What made Mexico so evil back in the 1840's, well before our Civil War, is that slavery was illegal there. Remember the Alamo?

If I am not the writer Lincoln and Twain were, I am at least a Humanist. I think that is what Mark Twain, if asked, would call himself nowadays. Nowadays it means persons like my parents and both sets of grandparents, who try to behave ethically without any expectation of rewards or punishments in an afterlife. They serve as best they can the only abstraction of which they have any real familiarity, which is their community.

What about Jesus? I say what one of my great grandfathers wrote, as follows: 'If so much of what Jesus said is ethically brilliant, and especially the Beatitudes, and "forgive us our trespasses as we forgive those who trespass against us," what can it matter whether he was God or not?'

My great grandfather's name was Clemens Vonnegut. Small world, small world.

This piquant coincidence is not a fabrication. I give you my word of honor that it is true.

Clemens Vonnegut called himself a 'Freethinker,' an antique word for Humanist. He was a hardware merchant in Indianapolis.

So, just as there was once a man named Adam who in Africa had all humanity in his loins, so, a hundred and twenty years ago, say, there was one man who was both Clemens and Vonnegut. I would have liked being such a person a lot. I only wish I could have been such a person tonight.

I claim no blood relationship with Samuel Clemens of Hannibal, Missouri. 'Clemens,' as a first name, is, I believe, like the name 'Clementine,' derived from the adjective 'clement.' To be clement is to be lenient and compassionate, or, in the case of weather, perfectly heavenly.

So there's weather again.

I am honorary President of the American Humanist Association. I succeeded the late, great science fiction writer Isaac Asimov in that completely functionless capacity. He had earned a doctorate in biochemistry, by the way.

We held a memorial service for Dr. Asimov a few years back, and at one point I said, 'Isaac is up in Heaven now.' That was the funniest thing I could have said to an audience of Humanists. It rolled them in the aisles. It was several minutes before order could be restored.

Should I ever happen to die, God forbid, I hope some of you will say, 'Kurt is up in Heaven now.'

That is my favorite joke.

And I thank you for your attention.

Two Poems

Alexis Lykiard

The People's Representative at Westminster

Unheralded and vilified, true pride of London town,
after weary years of protest camped upon the pavement,
victim of random assault, prey to police harassment,
and the petty spite of bureaucratic legislation,
Haw remains intransigent: neither backing off nor down.
His aim just to rile the conmen, cause them embarrassment,
win allies on this tented watch. Thus he keeps his station

under Big Ben, reproaches round the clock a Parliament
turned quite tame and passive. He's never yet seen fit to quit,
our stubbornly holy fool, but summons up some brazen wit,
forecasting glummer things to come, and speaks for the nation
on viewing the new wearer of the War Criminal's crown –
crony-catcher McBuggins, aka Gordon Brown.
Everyone should credit it: "Different arsehole, same old shit".

Howzat Haiku

[Not Cricket – or, Jack Hobbes in Iraq]

Our 'war'? Test of faith
That's nasty, British and fought
to the death – for what?

Star Wars Again

Noam Chomsky

In May, Professor Chomsky sent this letter to Jan Tamáš of the 'No Base' Initiative in the Czech Republic about the proposed anti-ballistic missile radar which the United States wishes to install there.

The installation of a missile defence system in Eastern Europe is, virtually, a declaration of war. Simply imagine how the US would react if Russia or China or Iran or in fact any foreign power dared even to think about placing a missile defence system at or near the borders of the United States, let alone carrying out such plans. In these unimaginable circumstances, a violent US reaction would be not only almost certain but also understandable for reasons that are simple and clear.

It is well known on all sides that missile defence is a first strike weapon. Respected US military analysts describe missile defence as 'not simply a shield but an enabler of US action'. It 'will facilitate the more effective application of US military power abroad'. 'By insulating the homeland from reprisal, [missile defence] will underwrite the capacity and willingness of the United States to "shape" the environment elsewhere.' 'Missile defence isn't really meant to protect America. It's a tool for global dominance.' 'Missile defence is about preserving America's ability to wield power abroad. It's not about defence. It's about offence. And that's exactly why we need it.' All quotes, from respected liberal and mainstream sources – who favour developing the system and placing it at the remote limits of US global dominance.

The logic is simple, and well understood. A functioning missile defence system informs potential targets that 'we will attack you as we please, and you will not be able to retaliate, so you cannot deter us'. The system is being marketed to Europeans as a defence against Iranian missiles. Even if Iran had nuclear weapons and long-range missiles, the chances of its using them to attack Europe are lower than the chances of Europe being hit by an asteroid, so if defence is the reason, the Czech Republic should be installing a system to defend the country from asteroids. If Iran were to indicate even the slightest intention of such a move, the country would be vapourized. The system is indeed aimed at Iran, but as a first strike weapon. It is a component of the escalating US threats to attack Iran, threats that are in themselves a serious violation of the UN Charter, though admittedly this issue does not arise in outlaw states.

When Gorbachev agreed to allow a unified Germany to join a hostile military alliance, he was accepting a very severe threat to Russian security, for reasons too familiar to review. In return, the US government made a firm pledge not to expand NATO to the East. The pledge was violated a few years later, arousing little comment in the West, but raising the threat of military confrontation. So-called 'missile defence' ratchets the threat of war a few notches higher. The 'defence' it provides is to increase the threat of aggression in the Middle East, with incalculable consequences, and the threat of terminal nuclear war.

Over half a century ago, Bertrand Russell and Alfred Einstein issued an extraordinary appeal to the people of the world, warning them that they face a choice that is 'stark and dreadful and inescapable: Shall we put an end to the human race; or shall mankind renounce war?' Accepting a so-called 'missile defence system' makes that choice, in favour of an end to the human race, perhaps in the not-too-distant future.

COMMUNICATION WORKERS UNION

End the occupation of Iraq

End the sanctions against the Palestinians

Free the elected leaders of Palestine

Billy Hayes
General Secretary

Jane Loftus
President

Manipulating the Security Council

Hans von Sponeck Interviewed by Silvia Cattori

Hans von Sponeck worked for the United Nations Development Programme for 32 years. In 1998, he was appointed United Nations Humanitarian Coordinator for Iraq. He resigned in March 2000 in protest at the sanctions on Iraq which were causing the Iraqi people great suffering. He gave this interview to Silvia Cattori of Voltairenet. Her questions and comments are printed in italic type, and Hans von Sponeck's replies are in ordinary type.

In your book A Different War: The UN Sanctions Regime in Iraq,[1] *you denounced openly the fact that the Security Council betrayed the principles of the UN Charter. Could you give us specific examples where the UN Secretariat behaved in an especially condemnable way?*

The Security Council must follow the UN Charter and it must not forget the Convention on the Rights of the Child and the general implications of these conventions. Moreover, if the Security Council knew that conditions in Iraq were inhuman – people of all ages were in deep trouble, not because of a dictator, but because of the policies around the 'oil for food programme' – and it decided not to act, or not to do enough to protect the people against the impact of its policy, then one can argue very easily that the Security Council is to be blamed, for example, for the very strong increase in the mortality rates in Iraq.

A definite example is that during the 1980s, under the government of Saddam Hussein, UNICEF identified 25 children per thousand under five years of age who were dying in Iraq for various reasons. During the years when sanctions were imposed, from 1990 to 2003, there was a sharp increase in mortality from 56 per thousand children under five years of age in the early 1990s to 131 per thousand under five years of age at the beginning of the new century. Now everyone can easily understand that this was due to the economic sanctions, so it is out of the question that the Security Council preferred to ignore the consequences of its policies in Iraq because of the pressure from major intervening parties including, and in particular, the United States and Great Britain.

How could the Security Council neglect to consider the fact that these sanctions allowed the superpowers to misuse their position and uniquely pursue their war objectives, when it voted for other resolutions, such as, for example, resolution 1559 which was particularly intended to provide the United States and Israel with a cover for future military strikes? Does that mean that the Security Council and the UN Secretariat, which are supposed to defend the people, have become mainly responsible for humanitarian catastrophes?

I would say that only those who are ignorant, or those who cannot accept the defeat, will continue to argue that the humanitarian drama in Iraq was largely not due – not exclusively but to a large extent – to an erroneous policy, a policy of punishment. The Iraqi people were punished for having accepted the government in Baghdad, even though they were completely innocent.

Our political leaders, who are present in all international bodies, knew perfectly well that these sanctions would have disastrous consequences. Does that mean that, by remaining silent, they have accepted innocent civilians being killed, tortured, and starved?

I would say that, unless the international community has a very bad memory, we cannot forget that either there was silence or there was connivance, support, or there was a deliberate effort to promote conditions of the kind that prevailed in Iraq during thirteen years of sanctions. Therefore, you get different levels of accountability, of political accountability. Not only the Prime Minister of Great Britain and the President of the United States and their governments are responsible, but others as well; Spain and Italy played a supportive role that means the former governments are responsible as well. Mr Aznar in Madrid and Mr Berlusconi in Italy are very much responsible for having contributed to the humanitarian disaster that evolved in Iraq. They will not accept this responsibility but the evidence is there.

If the manipulation of the Security Council by the United States is the main problem and if the US continues to commit crimes pretending that they have a UN mandate, what can be done to correct that unacceptable situation?

I think that this is a very important question. It is relevant for the debate about what kind of United Nations we need to protect the international community or to protect the 192 member governments from the danger that certain other governments misuse their authority, their information, their finances and their power to serve their own interest, but against the interests of peace, the interests of justice and the interests of mankind.

How did you react to the execution of Saddam Hussein and his co-defendants, sentenced to death by a tribunal established by the United States?

I would say, first of all, that I was not surprised. This was the ultimate objective of those in power in Baghdad and of those who occupy Iraq. It is impossible to defend

Saddam Hussein, but we can respond to the fact that there was no due process, that this was pretence. It was a tribunal that hid a prearranged death sentence under the cover of respectability. Saddam Hussein, like any other person, deserved the right to a fair trial, but he was not given a fair trial. And therefore I was upset by this obvious act, although we have international law, despite the fact that the European nations, the US and Canada as well as other western nations repeatedly express their intention to maintain justice, that they in fact did not protect justice.

You wrote to President Bush and asked him to free Tariq Aziz. Did you get any answer?

I did not get an answer. I wrote this letter because I know Mr Tariq Aziz. My predecessor and I both think he is a person with whom we had a correct relationship, a person who – despite what we read in the mainstream media – tried to care for the Iraqi people. He was ready and willing to consider proposals for the improvement of the humanitarian aid programme. From our perspective, from my perspective, he was a good person. I cannot judge what Mr Tariq Aziz did in Iraq outside my areas of responsibility, but all I want to ask for is that a person, who is ill, if for no other than humanitarian reasons, should be treated with dignity, should be allowed to obtain medical care while getting due process. Just like Saddam Hussein, Tariq Aziz deserved, and deserves, to be treated in accordance with international law, in accordance with The Hague and the Geneva Conventions. I object to the fact that over three years after he voluntarily turned himself in to the occupation forces, he has not even been charged, and still remains in custody while he is badly in need of medical care.

While the situation created by the occupation of Iraq is frightening, it is to be feared that the Resolution against Iran will be used by the United States to strike that country. The German Navy – formally under UN mandate – is in place in the Eastern Mediterranean. Is it because you know to what extent your country is involved in the projects of war of the United States that you recently wrote an open letter to Mrs Angela Merkel asking her to refuse all use of violence against Iran?

That is correct. I feel very strongly that, gradually, Germany and other European countries are getting involved in power policy defined in Washington by power-hungry people. This is becoming more serious because these power-hungry people begin to realize that they cannot, on their own, implement a policy of domination. So they need the help of other governments now, and these others seem to be Central European and Eastern European governments from Lithuania to Great Britain. They also try to politicise Nato and make it an instrument – to a large extent it has in fact already become a US instrument.

Therefore, just like any normal individual in this world, I cannot accept the attempts – supported by Chancellor Merkel during the Nato summit – to provide this military alliance with a political mission. Nato is an instrument of the Cold

War; for many years Nato was looking for a new mission, for a new role. The only thing the allies knew was that they have a military responsibility but, with the end of the Cold War in Europe, that responsibility no longer existed and was no longer necessary. So there was this desperate search for a new role.

I personally think that it is extremely dangerous that Nato now presents itself as a democratic instrument for western democracies while, in fact, it is a tool in the hands of the United States to implement the Project for the New American Century. Neoconservatives in the United States made this famous proposal in the 1990s – while the Bush administration converted it into its national security strategy of 2002 and subsequent years – and Nato is supposed to assist its implementation. The responsible politicians who met in Munich (in February 2007) should have rejected this concept.

Mr Vladimir Putin, the Russian President, for once did not mince his words and expressed plainly what many of us feel. Of course, those who follow a different agenda rejected his suggestions. However, there is a reality in what Mr Putin said.

I am convinced that, due to this militarised politicization of Nato, we have taken a big step backwards to what is not only a Cold War atmosphere between major powers, but also, and this is the tragedy, to an increase in defence spending in many countries including China, Russia, and Western Europe. This spending has already been greatly increased in numerous countries, and it can serve no other purpose than escalating the polarisation between different groups around the world.

The world beyond Central Europe and North America is no longer willing to accept a western one-sided policy. The public no longer accepts the requirements of last century's military and economic powers. Their days are over and, if we do not take this into account, we will only make things worse.

To me, the key words at the moment are dialogue and diplomacy. We have to accomplish this in a clearly multilateral spirit, not in the spirit of a superpower, which is anything but a superpower, be it economically, politically or morally, let alone ethically.

Even if there is a little bit of superpower spirit left in the United States because of its military power, it is not going to be enough to save the Pax Americana. Pax Americana is a thing of the past and the sooner we recognise this in Europe and prepare ourselves for multilateral cooperation – which is something different from the bilateral or Nato type cooperation – the better it will be.

Nato is taking part in wars of occupation – in contradiction to its own Charter – and, in collaboration with the CIA, it is involved in secret criminal operations. What I think of in this context are the abductions of suspects to secret prisons. If Europe continues to submit itself to and accepts the installation of American anti-missile systems in Nato member states, might this not lead to confrontation, or even to the return to the worst days of Cold War?

It is insane. There is no excuse, and Condoleezza Rice's argument according to which Russia had no reason to worry about ten anti-missile systems to be stationed in Poland and in the Czech Republic is so dishonest. If ten can be placed today, twenty might be placed tomorrow. The very fact that these anti-missile systems are positioned at the border of the former USSR, or Russia, is already enough to intensify the reasons for confrontation between Russia and the West, let alone China.

We are creating and we are shaping tomorrow's enemy. I, and with me many others around the globe, cannot accept this development. We do not count, however, we are weak, we are considered naïve, we are considered 'blue-eyed people', as the Americans have often called us, who do not understand the global vision.

If we are living in a democracy, then I have the right to understand this global vision, but I am not informed about it. I am just asked to rely on the good will and on the good intentions of a government like the one in Washington. But I cannot do so, we cannot do so, because we have been disappointed over and over again by misinformation, by brutal dishonesty, by power politics that only served one party. I am far from accepting this and, therefore, I regard the whole policy of convincing the Czech and Polish governments to have these anti-missile systems as extremely dangerous and misplaced. That is nothing but blatant and brutal power politics, which we do not need and which we will fight against. It is nothing that peace, future internationalism and the consolidation of nations and progress need – in the spirit of the UN Charter and other international laws.

You were in Kuala Lumpur in February, to attend a conference on war crimes. There was, in the West, very limited media coverage of this important event. If such meetings, which denounce the drift of Nato and the violations of the UN Charter, are ignored, how can a debate be opened for reforming these organisations? Don't you feel like you are speaking in a desert while the media, the UN, the States, go on lying and ignore your struggle?

One should not be discouraged by the fact that the media ignore us. Most of the time, when citizens tried to convince their leaders to change direction, they have been ignored. Should that be the end of the effort? I do not think so. The very fact that people, not just fools, not just misguided dreamers, but very realistic people who have an overall view on the world, who understand the political processes, come together to debate in a serious way the conditions and misuse of power, gives important evidence that the international conscience is alive, that an international conscience exists. Kuala Lumpur did not make it to the headlines. Hollywood makes it to the headlines, cheap emotionalism, and cheap quality media events like the Big Brother programme in London make headlines.

The fact that 5,000 people got together in Kuala Lumpur to discuss war as a crime, against the background of all the global sufferings that these illegal wars have caused, did not make it to the headlines is regrettable, but it should not make people less willing to speak out. Those who are concerned should notice it. Every one of us, as an individual, has a responsibility to assume, has to make his or her views known. In addition, I am sure that the Kuala Lumpur meeting has created more awareness in many circles around the world, which will ultimately be transferred into a greater resistance against these feint and selfish and one-sided policies that the West tries to enforce.

I am not anti-West, I am a 'Westerner', but that does not mean that I cannot critically look at the one-way street which has developed, the one-way highway on which international power, international trade, international culture are travelling. That, as I have said before, cannot continue because it is no longer acceptable, and Kuala Lumpur brought together people from all over the world, who are of the same opinion. So this has, I am sure, added to an awareness, and a willingness to invest time in order to make views known. And if that does not hit the headlines today and bring about a change immediately, it may do so tomorrow, and if it is not tomorrow, then the next day.

Voices like those of Mr Jimmy Carter and Mr John Dugard, who denounce the crimes of Israel in Palestine, voices like those of Mr Dennis Halliday[2] and yourself who put the finger on the UN's drifting off course in Iraq. All these voices demand immense respect. However, they are rare voices that can easily be marginalised by the political powers. Aren't you disappointed that hardly anybody, or only a few people at your level, follow your example and take a position against these state crimes and abuses?

Of course I am disappointed. You know, these days, every day, I am waiting anxiously for a senior American general, a senior American political personality to come out and say: enough is enough, I will not continue to support insanity, I will not support illegality, I will not support policies that have led us into deep difficulties and deep violations of anything that a civilised person should stand for. Of course, one is disappointed, but in view of what has happened during the last few decades, particularly during the years when Mr Bush has been in power, we cannot allow ourselves to be idle. This is an appeal for the international peace movement which should be oriented towards a better coordination, that is, much better networking, much more combined effort, much more joint declarations. People from all over the world should join hands and demonstrate to themselves and to the larger public that they have the firm intention not to accept what has led us into a world in which the gulf is wide open between those who have nothing – and that is a very, very large majority, over one billion people out of the six and a half billion people on our planet living with less than one dollar a day – and the top ten per cent who are living in unimaginable luxury and well being.

This cannot continue. And if some people who listen to our conversation may say 'here is really a very naïve person', and others say 'look, this is a communist, terrible, he is asking for equality for everybody', I will tell them 'no, I am not'. First of all, I do not think I am naïve, secondly, I do not think I am a communist in the traditional sense. I am a person who, in 32 years of work for the United Nations and beyond, has learned to accept the fact that all of us are not equal, but that all of us should have equal opportunities to develop our own contribution to peace. It is not a question of lack of money, there is plenty of money for everybody. But what is missing is the willingness to share the resources and to do more than pay lip service to this wonderful body of instruments that has been established by good people after the Second World War. Over the last sixty years, this body has tried to lay the basis for greater justice and for socioeconomic progress for everybody.

All the hope that you feed must make you suffer. You are well aware that, for the Muslim peoples whom the West is humiliating, the worst is still to come?

Of course. When you read and when you see what is happening in the Middle East, there is no single day on which you do not feel ashamed, you do not feel the humiliation that strikes us when we see these poor people suffering hard, people from Palestine to Iraq and in other parts of the Middle East as well. The human language is not, at least for me, capable of expressing the feelings that I really have. It is horrifying. I come from a country which has experienced and been the cause of this horrible Second World War. It lasted for five years, and we still talk about it. What about the many years in Iraq, thirty years of dictatorship, and thirteen years of sanctions, and now three and a half years of occupation: how much can an individual, how much can a nation endure? And if you see – I think of the universities I visited in Baghdad, Mustansiriya University, Baghdad College, Baghdad University – that these institutions, where young innocent people are supposed to prepare for life, were destroyed by bombs. When I was in Iraq, I saw people living peacefully in integrated neighbourhoods! I never heard a conversation like 'I am a Shiite, you are a Sunni, and you are a Turcoman' at that time.

Baghdad is the largest Kurdish city in the world with over one million Kurds, and there were many problems, for sure, there was a dictator, there were political murderers but, compared with what we see today, that was nothing. The sectarian confrontation that exists now was created due to an illegal war. And the threat towards the Al-Maliki government is the limit of dishonesty: 'If you do not bring security to Iraq, then we, the Americans, will reconsider to what extent we will continue our support'. What is this? Who established these kinds of conditions? Who is responsible for this chaos and the sectarian confrontation?

Western countries condemn Iran, that has signed the Nuclear Non-Proliferation Treaty, for a bomb that it does not have. They do not condemn Israel that did not sign this Treaty, and that has nuclear bombs. Choosing between Israel, that does not conceal preparing for waging a pre-emptive nuclear war, and Iran who wants to have a civil nuclear industry, is not Israel the one that is really threatening world peace, and is not Iran the target? How do you react to this denial of justice?

I have only one immediate response: it is a classic example of a double standard. We have a demand for a nuclear-free zone: it is the Security Council's resolution

687 of April 1991 which, in paragraph 14, calls for a nuclear-free zone for the complete Middle East. Israel has not even signed the Non-Proliferation Treaty. Iran may have intentions that are against the long-term international interests, but Iran has not yet passed the red line. Mr ElBaradei, the director of the International Atomic Energy Agency, did not say that Iran had passed that line. All he did was to say that Iran has not fully disclosed, not transparently enough, its intentions and that Iran has put more centrifuges into operation.

What an extraordinary demonstration of double standards, not to point the finger at Israel and others! What about Pakistan, what about India? And what about the US itself which is openly working on a new generation of nuclear weapons, totally in violation of the Non-Proliferation Treaty of which the United States is an initiator. So this is a disastrous double standard. If I were an Iranian, I would say: 'Sorry, take yourself the measures to put into practice what you say is the norm, and then we can talk; let's sit down at the table, at the same eye level, with no preconditions'.

I accept the Iranian demand for dialogue. I think it is absolutely the right thing to do. Iran says: 'you have a disagreement, so let's meet, but do not come and tell me before I can meet you, that I must have fulfilled certain conditions that you want me to fulfil; I am sorry, we come, we meet, we talk, and we lay the cards on the table'. And what we discover when we look at reality is a frightening attempt to keep up a double standard.

What message would you like to give to those political leaders who do not care about human rights, who wage wars and violate international and human rights? What message would you like to give to the populations who are, at present, exposed to the terror of occupying states? And what message would you like to give to those who oppose these wars but do not know how to stop them and are grieving over the inaction of the political parties?

To those who are violating human rights, I would say: you must live with your own guilty conscience, and how can you, in the light of all the evident damage, live with your guilty conscience? Don't you think that there are better ways to protect your interests by, at the same time, allowing others to benefit from existing opportunities?

To those who are victims and those who are concerned, I would say: never give up, just try your best, we all live in freedom, as healthy individuals, to make your contribution small, as it may be. If we gather for that aim, if we cooperate, if we network, if we try to make our views known to those in power, we can make a contribution. We can use our votes – those of us who live in countries with free elections – let us make use of our votes, but not in a mechanical way. For it is a great act of responsibility to cast a vote. Know your political candidates, put pressure on them, hold them accountable, check their records and, when there is a re-election, if you are not satisfied, encourage those who deserve your confidence to run for office. What else can we do?

Footnotes
1. *A Different Kind of War: The UN Sanctions Regime in Iraq,* Berghahn Books, 2006, ISBN 1845452224
2. Mr Dennis Halliday, former UN Assistant Secretary General and Humanitarian Coordinator for Iraq, predecessor of Mr Hans von Sponeck, whom the sanctions led to resign in protest in September 1998. He declared at that time: 'We are destroying an entire society (…). This is illegal and immoral.' His resignation was followed by that of Mr Hans von Sponeck, and, two days later, by that of Mrs Jutta Burghardt, in charge of the UN Food Programme, who joined the declaration of the preceding two.

With grateful acknowledgements to Current Concerns in Switzerland (www.currentconcerns.ch) and Voltairenet (www.voltairenet.org).

BURSTON STRIKE SCHOOL RALLY

Sunday 2nd September 2007
11am to 4.30pm, Church Green, Burston, nr. Diss, Norfolk

90th anniversary of the opening of the Strike School building and bicentenary of the abolition of trans-Atlantic slave trade

Guest Speakers:

BOB CROW, *RMT General Secretary*
TONY BENN
Prof MARY DAVIS, *labour & feminist historian*
COLLETTE CORK-HURST,
Unite - T&G Section National Secretary for Equalities

chaired by PAT d'CRUZ (Unite - T&G Section GEC) and STEVE HART (Unite - T&G Section Regional Secretary)

Live Music Session - folk / roots for a sunny afternoon

BILLY BRAGG HUCK // REDFLAGS

- Children's fun area including bouncy castle and playbus
- Food and beer tent
- Campaign and community stalls

∗ **Burston Strike School - The Longest Strike In History** ∗

Organised by the Unite - T&G Section (London, South East & East Anglia) with the support of SERTUC and the Burston Strike School Trustees

Polonium-210 in London

Zhores Medvedev

Zhores Medvedev is a geneticist and radiobiologist who worked at the Institute of Medical Radiology at Obninsk from 1963 to 1970, and later at the National Institute for Medical Research in London. He is the author of many books, including two on nuclear problems: Nuclear Disaster in the Urals *(1979) and* The Legacy of Chernobyl *(1990); as well as two published by Spokesman Books –* Secrecy of Correspondence is Guaranteed by Law *and* National Frontiers and International Scientific Co-operation *(both 1975). Dr Medvedev's new book,* Polonium-210 in London*, is expected to be published in Russian in Moscow at a later date. The contents have already been serialised in several Russian newspapers during the period February to May 2007.*

Illness without diagnosis

Alexander Litvinenko was taken to the Barnet Hospital on 3 November 2006 with suspected food poisoning or gut infection. During the first week he was treated with high doses of antibiotics, without proper tests for bacterial contamination. Two weeks later, an outside toxicologist suggested thallium poisoning. Large doses of the antidote, Prussian blue, began to be administered. Litvinenko was transferred to another hospital, to the haematology department, where treatment for thallium poisoning was continued, without any effect. It was only on 22 November that suspicion of possible radioactive poisoning emerged, and the samples of urine clearly showed a high level of alfa radiation. Samples were sent to a nuclear research laboratory where Polonium-210 was identified. There are several antidotes for polonium poisoning. But it was too late. Litvinenko was left with two hours to live.

The last few days of Litvinenko's life seemed to be more under the supervision of a public relations operation, rather than medicine. The world-wide distribution of photographs of the half-dressed patient in his hospital bed appeared to be a serious violation of medical ethics. In the case of radiation syndrome, with the immune system weakened, the patient should have been kept in sterile isolation. Instead, Litvinenko was made a celebrity with a constant stream of visitors. A powerful statement was prepared on his behalf two days before his death, when he was under heavy sedation. Litvinenko's Chechen friends invited an imam from the London Central Mosque to convert the sedated man to Islam, despite apparent objections from his wife and father. The exact immediate cause of Litvinenko's death has not yet been confirmed by the coroner's office. The post-mortem results remain classified.

Why Polonium-210?

Accidental poisoning with Polonium-210 of workers in the military and civilian branches of the nuclear industry are known, and the toxicology of polonium is well studied. However, there are no known previous cases of the deliberate use of polonium-210, or other alfa sources of radiation, for criminal purposes. This isotope is difficult to handle. Polonium metal is very hot and volatile. Commercial solutions of polonium salts are very expensive. Two to three Gigabecquerels (GBq) of polonium-210, which is a single human lethal dose for oral administration, cost about $2 million. This makes it unlikely that a free-lance or hired assassin would use it. This was the main reason for suspicion that the state was behind this crime. Because Russia is the main producer of Polonium-210, and because Litvinenko was a former Federal Security Service (FSB) officer, theories about the possible motives for his murder published in the general media tried to implicate Moscow or even Putin personally. Polonium-210 was, however, very convenient for the police. It left a very clear trail, which was followed. It was discovered that this trail leads to Moscow and Italy. Three persons were identified as carriers of polonium; Mario Scaramella, an Italian, and Andrey Lugovoy and Dmitry Kovtun, Russians.

Litvinenko – the escape from Russia

Since 1994, Litvinenko, as an officer of the Russian Federal Security Service, collaborated closely with the oligarch Boris Berezovsky. When Putin started to reduce the political power of the oligarchs in Russia, Berezovsky was one of the first victims. He quickly sold his main oil, car dealership and media assets in Russia for nearly $3 billion and left the country for good. In the process, Berezovsky also convinced Litvinenko to defect to the USA and subsidized preparations for the escape of Litvinenko and his family.

In October 2000, using false documents, Litvinenko managed to reach Turkey via Ukraine and Georgia. However, the US Embassy in Ankara refused to grant him an entry visa. The CIA officer at the embassy interviewed Litvinenko, but was not impressed by his explanations. Berezovsky sent his assistant, Alex Goldfarb, to Turkey apparently to solve the problem. Goldfarb worked out a plan to return to Moscow via London. While at Heathrow, Litvinenko refused to board the connecting flight to Moscow and asked for political asylum in the United Kingdom. He was allowed to stay, while the application was considered.

Russian security officer in England
Attempts at writing

Berezovsky seemingly wanted Litvinenko in the United States to co-author the book *Blowing up Russia: The Secret Plot to Bring Back KGB Terror*, which he had personally sponsored. It was under preparation by Yuri Feltshtinsky, a Jewish émigré who had lived in New York since 1978. The book, apparently written to compromise Putin, was nearly finished. However, Feltshtinsky, a historian, was thought not to be a credible author on his own. With a real FSB officer as co-author, the book might enjoy much wider acceptance. However, the book, which was published in Russian in Latvia in 2001, and in English in 2002, was a failure, mainly because of the lack of documentation and factual evidence. Berezovsky sponsored Litvinenko's second book, *The Lubianka Criminal Gang,* about the Federal Security Service. A professional journalist was brought from Moscow to help with the writing. Alex Goldfarb wrote a long 'Preface' for the book, putting it in the same class as Alexander Solzhenitsyn's *Gulag Archipelago.* However, this book, which was published in Russian in 2002, was also a failure. It was not translated into English or other languages.

Since his arrival in London in October 2000, Litvinenko reportedly received a generous grant of £60,000 per year via the Foundation for Civil Liberties, which was administered by Alex Goldfarb. After the failure of the second book there were no new projects for Litvinenko, and the grant from the Foundation came to an end. From 2004, Litvinenko was left without a regular income. He had to start earning a living.

Berezovsky and Goldfarb's 'Fund for Civil Liberties'

Boris Berezovsky was charged in Russia with fraud, tax evasion and other offences. The warrant for his arrest and extradition was also issued by Interpol. As a person with political asylum status he was unable to use his considerable wealth for direct support of the opposition to Putin. However, he established the 'Foundation for Civil Liberties' with an initial fund of $25 million and appointed Alex Goldfarb as its Director. This Foundation opened offices in Moscow, Kiev, Tbilisi and other cities of the former Soviet Union and became very active in support of oppositional movements.

Alexander Goldfarb, now an American citizen, graduated from Moscow University in 1969. From 1969 until 1975, he was a junior scientist and graduate student at the top secret Kurchatov Institute of Atomic Energy. His doctoral thesis project was on enzymes of DNA and RNA synthesis, and he was attached to the Radiobiology Division of the Institute. In 1975, Goldfarb unexpectedly applied for emigration to Israel and was granted an exit visa. He worked at the Weizman Institute in Tel Aviv until 1980. From 1980 to 1982, he worked in the Federal Republic of Germany and, since 1983, at Columbia University in New York as Assistant Professor. From 1991 to 1997, Goldfarb was chairman of the Moscow Bureau of the Soros Foundation, and distributed Soros grants to many academic projects. He also became head of the molecular biology laboratory of the Public Health Research Institute at Newark, New Jersey, in the United States, where he works as a biochemist. This laboratory has a large team of Russian scientists and publishes many research papers jointly with Moscow institutes, including the former Kurchatov Institute radiobiology division.

Scotland Yard detectives move along the radioactive trail

Polonium-210 gave the police a unique opportunity to follow the radioactive trail. Their discoveries were widely reported by press and TV. More than 20 places in London, including Berezovsky's own office, were found to be contaminated with Polonium-210. Radioactivity was found on British Airways planes that flew from and to Moscow in October and November. The highest levels of contamination were found to be associated with hotel rooms, bars and restaurants which were linked to three persons, Scaramella, Lugovoy and Kovtun. Polonium-210 was also found in Hamburg, and associated with Kovtun's visit to Germany on 28 to 31 October. However, the radioactive trail contained two peaks, the first dated 15-16 October, the second dated 30 October to 3 November. This discovery led to the theory that Litvinenko was poisoned twice, first in the middle of October and then again on 1 November. The first dose, it is suggested, was not sufficient to kill him. There were some spots of contamination which did not fit the theory.

The main puzzle was Mario Scaramella, an Italian friend of Litvinenko. He was invited to London for tests and found to have massive contamination with polonium. A few days later it was reported that only 'traces' were found. Scaramella returned to Italy. Italian doctors found polonium-210 in his body. There were no contacts between Scaramella and Lugovoy or Kovtun, the main initial suspects. Scaramella was invited again to London and was admitted to the same hospital where Litvinenko had been treated. Polonium-210 contamination was found, but the levels were not disclosed. The Italian spent nearly two weeks in hospital. He was allowed to return to Italy on 24 December. On arrival in Italy he was arrested and charged on several counts not related to radioactivity. He was put in jail and the bail application was refused. Apparently nobody wanted to interview him about polonium or Litvinenko. Scotland Yard detectives wanted to interview Lugovoy and Kovtun in Moscow. However, when these interviews were granted, both men were in a radiological clinic with symptoms of radiation syndrome, light in the case of Lugovoy and acute in the case of Kovtun. The interviews were carried out in hospital. Both men were classified as 'witnesses', not 'suspects'. From 30 October to 3 November, Lugovoy had been in London with his wife, two daughters and son. Scotland Yard's longest interview was with Lugovoy's wife. Details of these interviews have not been disclosed.

Scaramella remained in prison and nobody wanted to press charges. In April 2007, he was transferred to hospital, under guard, with a heart attack, high blood pressure, hair loss and other health problems. In June , whilst still ill, he was placed under house arrest.

Litvinenko in London – Attempts at consultancy businesss

The first theory of Kremlin involvement which received the attention of Scotland Yard, and wide coverage in the media, was reportedly suggested by Yuri Shvets, a former Major in the KGB who defected. He had served as an intelligence officer in Washington under diplomatic cover. Shvets knew Litvinenko and Scaramella. He was a member of the Berezovsky-Goldfarb group, involved in several projects. Yuri Shvets apparently told British detectives who flew to Virginia, where he lives, that he and Litvinenko jointly prepared a report investigating Victor Ivanov, deputy head of President Putin's administration. The 'risk assessment report', running to eight pages, was commissioned by a well-known British company which was considering an investment worth 'dozens of millions of dollars' into an industrial project which was under the supervision of Victor Ivanov. The Litvinenko and Shvets report apparently described Victor Ivanov as a former KGB general and Stalinist 'old guard'. The expected investment was cancelled. A substantial fee (some papers talked about $100,000) was paid to Litvinenko and Shvets. According to this theory the murder of Litvinenko was possibly revenge for the lost contract. Lugovoy, as a former KGB major himself, was alleged to have carried out the order. This theory was apparently supported by Berezovsky, Goldfarb, Feltshtinsky and other members of Berezovsky's circle. However, Scotland Yard seemingly did little to pursue it. The 'risk assessment report' was found. It was poorly written and contained information easily available from Russian language internet sources. It was delivered to the British company on 20 September 2006. It is not clear how Ivanov was supposed to have been able to read it, and why polonium-210 should have been used.

Litvinenko in London – from consultancy to blackmail?

The second theory that received prominence in *The Observer* on 3 December, which was also apparently not pursued by Scotland Yard, tried to explain Litvinenko's fate by his blackmailing activities. Yulia Svetlichnaya, 33, a Russian journalist and graduate student at the University of Westminster in London, provided information on Litvinenko's apparent attempt to offer her a kind of partnership in blackmailing wealthy 'New Russians' who live in London and do not want to disclose the sources of their wealth. These can often be linked to their Communist, KGB or even criminal backgrounds. Litvinenko apparently was particularly excited about the 'Yukos dossier' concerning a Russian oil company. Most the members of the Yukos management fled Russia for the West after Mikhail Khodorkovsky's trial in Moscow, in 2004. The main co-owner of Yukos, Leonid Nevzlin, settled in Israel. He was in charge of substantial capital, thought to be some $7 billion, distributed among many offshore accounts and administered through the Gibraltar branch of the MENATEP bank. MENATEP was a Russian bank founded by Khodorkovsky and Nevzlin in 1993, which bought the Yukos company in 1996 at one of the privatization auctions of the Yeltsin era. MENATEP became a financial section of Yukos.

The obvious implication of *The Observer* story was that, if Litvinenko did indeed start his blackmailing plans, one of his targets might have reacted by silencing him for good. However, it became known that Litvinenko flew to Israel in September 2006 to deliver 'The Yukos dossier' personally to Nevzlin. Nevzlin acknowledged this unexpected visit, but said that the 'Yukos dossier' had been returned to the British Embassy in Israel. Litvinenko received British citizenship on 12 October 2006. His trip to Israel needed visa and Home Office travel documents available for stateless residents of the United Kingdom, and the approval of police necessary for political-asylum-protected refugees. The content of the 'Yukos dossier' was not disclosed.

Why did Scotland Yard close the investigation?
Who poisoned Litvinenko? The British press verdict

Scotland Yard's anti-terrorist branch formally closed the Litvinenko case at the end of January 2007 and sent it to the Crown Prosecution Service. There were some reports that the British government considered a request for the extradition of Lugovoy and

Kovtun from Moscow. Later, Kovtun was droppped as a main suspect apparently because he had been a military intelligence officer, not KGB. There were no new interviews or investigations of possible motives behind this crime. A team of Russian detectives arrived in London in April 2007 to work on the Russian Prosecutor's case which was entitled 'The murder of Russian citizen Litvinenko and the attempted murder of Russian citizen Dmitry Kovtun'. Russian detectives interviewed Berezovsky and some members of the Yukos management who live in London. The main focus of the Russian investigation was on the financial details of Litvinenko's life in the United Kingdom. Meanwhile, the Russian Federation Prosecution Service somehow found, in December 2006, entirely new materials on Yukos and ordered a new trial of the Yukos managers Mikhail Khodorkovsky and Platon Lebedev, who were serving nine year sentences in a Siberian camp. At the beginning of December 2006, both men were transferred to the regional capital and put in jail. The estimated sum of hidden capital managed by MENATEP was raised to $25 billion.

Litvinenko in London
The trade in confidential FSB documents or blackmail – what is more dangerous?

Very poor knowledge of English made it difficult for Litvinenko to do independent consultancy work for British companies. He was apparently negotiating for some 'risk assessment' or 'due diligence' reports on behalf of two of his new friends who were members of Berezovsky's circle, but dependent also on free-lance income. They were Yuri Shvets, graduate of Moscow University and the KGB Academy economy section, and Evgeny Limarev, son of a KGB general and graduate of the Moscow Institute of International Relations. They were reportedly both experts in computer penetration work. Limarev settled in France where he created an Internet site, *RusGlobus,* for Berezovsky. Shvets and Litvinenko also did some work for Mario Scaramella, who was employed by the Italian Parliamentary Commission to study a part of the smuggled KGB archive, known as the 'Mitrokhin Papers', apparently in search of links between the KGB and socialist and communist politicians and academics in Italy. This study was commissioned by Prime Minister Berlusconi, who was reportedly looking for some compromising materials about Romano Prodi, his main rival. The Italian file of the 'Mitrokhin Papers' was sent by the Secret Intelligence Service (SIS) from London, where Vasily Mitrokhin lived after the collapse of the Soviet Union. The documents were in Russian, and this necessitated the assistance of Litvinenko and Shvets. Scaramella paid Litvinenko a modest fee for this work. He also used to invite Limarev as well, but had to fly to the United States when it was necessary to get Shvets' opinion. When Romano Prodi won the elections in Italy he liquidated the 'Mitrokhin Commission'.

Since 2005, Litvinenko had also been trying to sell the British media some secret papers that originated from his former FSB special unit. Apparently, he was able to penetrate some FSB sites, probably because he knew secret passwords or had an accomplice inside the service. However, these documents (I was able to read some of them) were mostly about corruption, ethnic mafia clans and organised criminal gangs. They were of little interest to the British press or British intelligence and their circulation was limited. In 2004, both Litvinenko and Shvets were apparently employed by the Foundation for Civil Liberties to research tape recordings of President Leonid Kuchma of Ukraine. These were known as the 'Melnichenko Tapes'. The alleged attempt to use these tapes for blackmail apparently failed.

The 'Yukos dossier', which Litvinenko was excited about in May 2006, was under preparation for a few months. Limarev apparently did some research on the foreign assets of Yukos, while Shvets was said to be an expert in finding offshore accounts. Litvinenko, as a former FSB operations officer, did the practical work, delivering the 'dossier' personally to Nevzlin in Tel Aviv.

The group radioactive poisoning – Litvinenko was one of several victims

From 1995 to 1999, Litvinenko's job in a special unit of the FSB, which had been created to fight organised criminal gangs, gave him practical knowledge of blackmail. The extortion of money from gang leaders or 'godfathers' was part of the operation. He knew that the messenger to the mafia territory should be protected. The messenger is a member of the group, and sensitive information will be disclosed if the messenger finds himself in trouble. However, both Limarev and Shvets, who did some research on Yukos, would hardly have been able to disclose the 'dossier', if attempts to silence the messenger were taken. Litvinenko delayed a trip to Israel several times. However, when he met Andrey Lugovoy in London in July 2006, he thought that he had found a reliable partner. Litvinenko and Lugovoy were friends since 1995 when they both provided security for Berezovsky in Russia. In 1996, Lugovoy was a KGB bodyguard for Berezovsky's travels to Chechnya, while Litvinenko was investigating an attempt on Berezovsky's life, in 1994. In 2004, when Litvinenko resumed contacts with Lugovoy in London, his friend was already a wealthy businessman in Russia and the owner of several companies worth about $100 million. One of his companies, 'The Ninth Wave', provided security services.

Large international corporations such as Yukos employ professional security units to protect their management and interests. These professionals would deal with blackmail as well. They apparently knew that Litvinenko, who arrived in Tel Aviv in September, was a member of a group. To silence him might mean the release of information damaging to the interests of Yukos. Was it necessary to neutralise the whole group for real practical results? In September, after his return to London from Israel, Litvinenko was under close observation. When stakes are measured in billions of dollars, professional expenses of this kind are an easy part of the exercise. The problem was the task. The persons probably identified as possible suspects lived in different countries: Italy, Russia, France, the United States. If one of them was to be neutralised, the others would act. Neither firearms nor chemical poisons would give enough time. Only radioactive poisoning can do the job. Among radioactive isotopes, only alfa sources escape the airport radiation monitors. Among alfa emitters, only polonium-210 has the necessary qualities:

minimal gamma impulses, long half-life, and a well-studied toxicology. It is also commercially available. A person poisoned by polonium is 'walking dead' for nearly two weeks, without suspecting the danger. When he is taken to hospital, the discovery of alfa radiation is difficult. His home or flat can be cleared of sensitive documents without any undue haste. We now know that four men received substantial amounts of polonium-210: Litvinenko, Kovtun, Lugovoy and Scaramella. This was well above the possible 'contamination' level. Limarev's house in the French Alps was broken in to, during his trip to Italy, and some documents were stolen. Apparently nobody tried to find out why. After Litvinenko's death, Limarev and all the members of his family went into hiding for two weeks. Yuri Shvets, as a professional spy, probably took better protective measures.

Who poisoned Litvinenko and Kovtun? The theory

The propaganda and publicity effect of Litvinenko's death was accidental. It was likely that polonium poisoning would never be discovered, and no links identified

A Timeline of Events

On 21 November 2000, at a meeting with Russian President Vladimir Putin in Moscow, British Prime Minister Tony Blair promised to be an intermediary between Russia and the United States regarding a missile defense system. In February 2001, London took the side of the US on the issue.

In August 2001, Rafael Bravo, an employee of the company BAE Systems Avionics, was arrested for spying for Russia.

In March 2002, another employee of BAE, Ian Parr, was caught attempting to pass information to Russia about a new missile.

On 12 September 2002, a London court denied a Russian request for the extradition of businessman Boris Berezovsky. Similar decisions were made regarding former LogoVAZ Chief Executive Yulia Dubova and Chechen envoy Ahmed Zakayev.

On 7 June 2004, the Russian Foreign Ministry announced that the British Council was engaged in commercial activities in Russia and that it could face fines. After the issue was discussed by Mr. Putin and Mr. Blair at the G8 summit in the US on 10 June, the complaints were dropped.

On 18 March 2005, a London court refused to extradite former Yukos employees Dmitry Maruyev and Natalia Chernysheva, and, on 23 December 2005, a similar request for the extradition of Yukos vice president and deputy managing chairman Alexander Temerko was denied.

In August 2005, British sailors participated in the rescue of an AS-28 submarine off the coast of Kamchatka and were rewarded by Vladimir Putin personally.

In January 2006, several British diplomats in Moscow were accused of espionage and the illegal financing of non-commercial organizations.

between several deaths in different countries and at different dates. If the dose had been only slightly higher for Litvinenko, his fate would not have been such a sensation.

The assassins in blackmail plots do not like too much attention because it means more intensive investigation. The Russian Procurator General received some important materials after Litvinenko's death. When his office opened a criminal case on the murder of Litvinenko and the attempted murder of Kovtun, it immediately combined this with the Yukos criminal case which had existed since 2003, when Khodorkovsky and Lebedev were arrested, and Nevzlin fled to Israel. The Russian Procurator reportedly made Nevzlin the main 'suspect' for the Litvinenko and Kovtun investigation. Litvinenko died on 23 November 2006. Ten days later, the former directors of Yukos, Khodorkovsky and Lebedev, who, as we have seen, were serving sentences of nine years in an East Siberian camp near the uranium mining town of Krasnokamensk, were transferred to the regional capital, Chita, and put into a local prison. Their lawyers in Moscow were informed that a new trial was forthcoming.

In July 2006, British Ambassador to Russia Anthony Brenton attended a forum organized by the opposition coalition The Other Russia, after which the pro-Kremlin youth movement Nashi carried out several protests demanding apologies for the 'speech before the fascists'.

On 12 October 2006, the British Foreign Office included Russia on its list of countries that are human rights violators.

On 23 November 2006, Alexander Litvinenko, who had been granted political asylum in the United Kingdom, died in London after being poisoned with polonium-210.

On 22 May 2007, British prosecutors charged Russian former FSB officer Andrei Lugovoy with Mr. Litvinenko's murder.

On 6 June 2007, Tony Blair said that he would not recommend investment in Russia to British companies.

On 16 June, the British government awarded official honours to a defector named Oleg Gordievsky and the judge Timothy Workman, who turned down Russia's extradition request for Boris Berezovsky and Ahmed Zakayev.

On 25 June, the FSB announced that charges had been filed against the former head of the Russian tax police, Vyacheslav Zharko, who was recruited by British intelligence.

On 5 July, the Russian General Prosecutor's Office announced (informally) that it would not hand over Mr. Lugovoy.

On 10 July, the Russian General Prosecutor's Office formally announced its refusal of the British government's request to extradite Mr. Lugovoy.

Source: *Kommersant,* 12 July 2007

The murder of Litvinenko remains unresolved. It seems that this may suit both sides in the investigation. The Russian Procurator is unlikely to acknowledge that he was a beneficiary of the blackmail plot. The Metropolitan Police in Britain, it seems, will not try to follow the blackmail theory suggested in *The Observer*. Is this lead too sensitive politically? Dmitry Kovtun fortunately survived the effects of polonium. But the fate of Mario Scaramella, who was transferred to hospital in April 2007, is still uncertain.

Polonium-210 as radiopoison – toxicology and radiobiology

The organisers who were behind this operation knew some of the basics of radiobiology. However, they studied only a limited amount of literature, probably via the internet. They were in a hurry. Internet sources do not cover the literature published between 1960 and 1980. In these early studies it was found that polonium-210, if ingested, is very poorly absorbed into the blood stream. Only about five or six per cent of ingested polonium passes through the intestine wall. 90 to 95 per cent is removed via the faeces without any damage. Alfa radiation does not reach the stem cells layer of the intestine. All studies of the toxicity of polonium-210 during the last 20 to 25 years were carried out using intravenous injections. To do otherwise would have been a waste of money. The first poisoning of several men, carried out in the middle of October, was a failure due to insufficient doses. The second attempt was not easy to make. The dynamic of polonium in different tissues, and the results of the post-mortem, might solve the problem of dates. But it is not likely that the results of such a study will be published. Experts have already published the graphs of the possible distribution of polonium-210 in Litvinenko's tissues. When it will be possible to compare them with the real picture, nobody knows.

Postscript
The decision of the Crown Prosecution Service, as reported on 22 May 2007, to charge Lugovoy with the murder of the former 'Russian Spy', Alexander Litvinenko, was perhaps inevitable, but was it irrelevant? Was it embarrassing just to close the case without charging anyone? Was it the case that the Crown Prosecution Service could not leave the problem for the next British government, which took office in June? Lugovoy had already been accused many times by the press, TV and even in books published in London. Can a 'fair trial' be possible in these circumstances?

Bakers, Food & Allied Workers Union

*Suuporting workers in struggle
Wherever they may be.*

Joe Marino   General Secretary
Ronnie Draper   President
Jackie Mander   Vice President

Stanborough House,
Great North Road,
Stanborough,
Welwyn Garden City,
Hertfordshire. AL8 7TA
Phone 01707 260150& 01707 259450
www.bfawu.org

Routledge Classics

Get inside one of the greatest minds of the Twentieth Century

BERTRAND RUSSELL TITLES

History of Western Philosophy
Bertrand Russell

'Should never be out of print.'
– *The Evening Standard*

792pp: 0-415-32505-6: **£12.99**

Sceptical Essays
Bertrand Russell

With a new preface by **John Gray**

'Bertrand Russell wrote the best English prose of any twentieth-century philosopher.' – *The Times*

240pp: 0-415-32508-0: **£9.99**

In Praise of Idleness
Bertrand Russell

With a new introduction by **Anthony Gottlieb**

'There is not a page that does not provoke argument and thought.'
– *The Sunday Times*

192pp: 0-415-32506-4: **£8.99**

Why I Am Not a Christian
Bertrand Russell

With a new introduction by **Simon Blackburn**

'Devastating in its use of cold logic.'
– *The Independent*

272pp: 0-415-32510-2: **£9.99**

Power
Bertrand Russell

With a new introduction by **Samuel Brittan**

'Extremely penetrating analysis of human nature in politics.'
– *The Sunday Times*

288pp: 0-415-32507-2: **£9.99**

(New)
The Conquest of Happiness
Bertrand Russell

With a new preface by **A.C. Grayling**

'He writes what he calls common sense, but is in fact uncommon wisdom.'
– *The Observer*

200pp: 0-415-37847-8: **£9.99**

an **informa** business

www.routledge.com/classics

Available from all good bookshops

THE BERTRAND RUSSELL PEACE FOUNDATION
DOSSIER

2007   Number 25

THE QUARTET'S 'IMPOSSIBLE DEMANDS' OF HAMAS

These excerpts are taken from Alvaro de Soto's confidential End of Mission Report to the United Nations, dated May 2007. It was leaked shortly after he resigned as the United Nations Special Co-ordinator for the Middle East Peace Process, the Personal Representative of the Secretary-General to the Palestine Liberation Organization and the Palestinian Authority, and as UN Envoy to the Quartet, the Middle East grouping dominated by the United States which also includes the European Union and Russia.

Barely five days after the 25 January 2006 elections, the Palestinians received an icy shower in the form of a pre-programmed Quartet meeting in London on 30 January 2006. Just as the dominant issue in September had been whether Hamas should participate in the elections, in January it was how to handle the result.

Not that the Palestinians were totally unprepared for the shock: warning shots had been fired across their bow in two statements, both issued after teleconferences between the Principals, issued on 28 December 2005 and on 26 January 2006, the day after the elections. In the first, the Quartet called on all those 'who want to be part of the political process' to 'renounce violence, recognize Israel's right to exist, and disarm', and 'expressed its view that a future Palestinian Authority Cabinet should include no member who was not committed to the principles of Israel's right to exist in peace and security and an unequivocal end to violence and terrorism.' In the second, also issued after a teleconference, the Quartet said: 'A two-state solution to the conflict requires all participants in the democratic process to renounce violence and terror, accept Israel's right to exist, and disarm, as outlined in the Road Map.'

Yet in a 13 January meeting, I had gathered the impression that, though the United States had clearly decided who were 'the bad guys', they were not entirely averse to the approach, which I floated. This approach, drawing on the flexibility of Russia and the UN – those members of the Quartet unencumbered by legislative constraints regarding dealings with Hamas – would have been designed to encourage Hamas to continue moving in the direction taken when it decided to participate in the elections.

What I had in mind was that the Quartet could adopt a *common but differentiated* approach towards Hamas and the new government, and I recommended to UNHQ that we avoid tying our hands in ways that we might come to regret later. I also said that, whereas we had to acknowledge that the United States and the European Union had real domestic constraints with regard to assistance to a government involving members of a movement listed by them as a terrorist organization, they should in turn acknowledge that a group that is likely to hold a high percentage of seats in the Legislature could not be effectively dealt with by pressure and isolation alone, that Hamas was evolving and could evolve still more, that if we are to encourage that evolution some channel of dialogue would be necessary, and that for the UN to play such a role, as it had done successfully in many cases elsewhere in the world, it had to be given some space. I also proposed that, regardless of what position it took regarding the new Palestinian dispensation, the Quartet should register concern about Israel's creation of facts on the ground, which impinge on the viability – indeed, let's not beat around the bush, the very achievability – of a future Palestinian state, and agree to become more explicit about the need for negotiations and convergence on the end-goal of the Road Map process …

I could not erase what the Quartet had already said on 28 December. However, to me, it was one thing to take positions before the elections, when we all assumed an outcome that would preserve Fateh's majority, and another to take positions in the face of an outright Hamas victory. The people had spoken in free and fair elections whose holding had been encouraged by the international community, and their wishes should be respected. We had an entirely new, unforeseen situation before us, and we should adjust our reaction accordingly. The 26 January statement, which in effect echoed the one of 28 December, undercut me seriously in that respect

On 29 January we received a draft statement prepared by the United States that would have had the Quartet, in effect, decide to review all assistance to the new Palestinian Authority government unless its members adhered to three principles: nonviolence, recognition of Israel, and acceptance of previous agreements and obligations including the Road Map. It was quite clear that the Secretary-General could not speak for donors. As a stopgap, therefore, with the approval of the Secretary-General, I proposed that either the reference to the review of assistance should be deleted altogether or the decision should be taken only by the donor members of the Quartet.

I had arrived in London bereft of guidance from UNHQ in response to recommendations on the eve of the Quartet Principals meeting scheduled on 30 January, and was only able to consult with the Secretary-General at a rather late stage.

The Envoys met at 10am on 30 January in preparation for the Principals' meeting in the evening. I was subjected to a heavy barrage from Welch and Abrams [the US representatives], including ominous innuendo to the effect that if the Secretary-General didn't encourage a review of projects of UN agencies and programmes it could have repercussions when UN budget deliberations took place on Capitol Hill. This question was resolved when the US stepped back from insisting on a decision by the Quartet on the matter, and settled for language – proposed, incidentally, by the US legal advisor, a veteran of Camp David and other US Middle East efforts – under which the Quartet merely *'concluded* that it was inevitable that future assistance to any new government would be reviewed by donors against that government's commitment to the principles of nonviolence, recognition of Israel, and acceptance of previous agreements and obligations, including the Road Map'.

Despite the constraints under which I was operating, I pleaded with the Envoys for an approach that would be more compatible with the United Nations playing the role which comes naturally to us as explained above. I was weakened by the willingness expressed by both my European Union and Russian colleagues, at the outset, to accept the language proposed by the United States. I found myself arguing alone for formulations that would be more consistent with the Quartet's support for Abu Mazen's strategy of co-operation, firstly, and, secondly, more conducive to conveying to Hamas the message that the international community recognizes and welcomes the movement that they have made by participating in the elections and respecting the electoral rules of the game and by and large respecting the *'Hudna'* [ceasefire], and that we earnestly hope that such movement will continue so that the international community can maintain the support it has always provided to the Palestinians. Predictably, I was unsuccessful in these endeavours; hence the undesirably punitive-sounding tone of the 30 January statement from which we have not succeeded in distancing ourselves to this day, and which effectively transformed the Quartet from a negotiation-promoting foursome guided by a common document (the Road Map) into a body that was all but imposing sanctions on a freely elected government of a people under occupation as well as setting unattainable preconditions for dialogue.

The impact of Quartet policy on the Palestinians and on prospects for a two state solution

The devastating consequences of the Quartet position have been well documented, including in UN Security Council briefings. Those consequences were, in fact, predicted by the Office of the United Nations Special Co-ordinator (UNSCO) in a paper that we circulated to Quartet partners before the London meeting on the institutional implications of pulling the financial plug on the Palestinian Authority. The precipitous decline of the standard of living of Palestinians, particularly but by no means exclusively in Gaza, has been disastrous, both in humanitarian terms and in the perilous weakening of Palestinian institutions. International assistance, which had been gradually shifting to development and institutional reform, has reverted largely to the humanitarian. The service-delivering capacity of the Palestinian Authority, consisting of the thousands of doctors, nurses and teachers, employees of the Palestinian Authority, who provide the bulk of medical care and education, has suffered tremendously. Perversely, this regression has made the already critical role of United Nations Relief and Works Agency (UNRWA), as well as other UN agencies, even more crucial to the well-being of the Palestinians.

The underpinnings for a future Palestinian state have been seriously undermined, and the capacity of the Palestinian security apparatus to establish and maintain law and order, to say nothing of putting an end to attacks against Israel, has diminished tremendously – hardly surprising, given that the security forces who would have to risk their lives to achieve these goals haven't been being paid regular salaries. Thus the steps taken by the international community with the presumed purpose of bringing about a Palestinian entity that will live in peace with its neighbour Israel have had precisely the opposite effect.

Beyond the damage wrought in terms of international assistance, which in the final analysis is voluntary, there is that which has been inflicted by Israel, notwithstanding its responsibilities to the population, under international law, as occupying power: not just the killings of hundreds of civilians in sustained heavy incursions and the destruction of infrastructure, some of it wanton such as the surgical strikes on the only power plant, as well as bridges in Gaza; also the cessation of transfer to the Palestinian Authority, since February 2006, of the VAT and customs duties which Israel collects, under the Paris Protocol signed with the PLO pursuant to the Oslo Accords, on behalf of the Palestinians. This is money collected from Palestinian exporters and importers. It is Palestinian money. In normal circumstances it adds up to a full one third of Palestinian income. It is the main source of payment of salaries to Palestinian Authority employees. While the international community demands from the Palestinian government that it should accept 'previous agreements and obligations', Israel deprives the Palestinian Authority of the capacity to deliver basic services to the Palestinian population in violation of one such 'previous agreement', as well as its International Humanitarian Law obligations regarding the welfare of the population whose land it occupies.

Israel's cutoff of the main source of income of the Palestinian Authority was never intended by three of the Quartet members. The UN (myself) was the first to call on Israel not to do this, the very day that the decision was communicated to international representatives. The European Union has since repeatedly called on Israel to resume transfer; the sums withheld surely add up to the high hundreds of millions of dollars by now. However, the Quartet has been prevented from pronouncing on this because the United States, as its representatives have intimated to us, does not wish Israel to transfer these funds to the Palestinian Authority. It is interesting that in a recent interview in the *Financial Times* Secretary Rice was quoted as saying 'I do think that there are certain responsibilities that come with governing and that Hamas has not lived up to those because it has been unable to deliver because it is isolated from the international system because it will not give up violence. So there's a consequence to being in power and being unable to deliver.' One wonders whether it is credible to judge the ability of a government to deliver when it is being deprived of its largest source of income, to which it is indubitably entitled by virtue of an agreement endorsed by the Security Council, by the State which largely controls the capacity of that government and its people to generate income. In fact, the Palestinian

Authority government is being expected to deliver without having make-or-break attributes of sovereignty such as control of its borders, the monopoly over the use of force, or access to natural resources, let alone regular tax receipts.

In general, the other consequence of Quartet policy has been to take all pressure off Israel. With all focus on the failings of Hamas, the Israeli settlement enterprise and barrier construction has continued unabated. (In the same time period, the idea has also gained ground in Western public opinion and even some Arab governments that the problem in the region is Iran and the 'Shia crescent' – a framing device which tends to mute attention to the Palestinian issue.)

Palestinian realignment and the formation of a National Unity Government

Soon after the elections, Hamas expressed its desire to establish a broad-based government. The reactions in Fateh were mixed, but before the idea could advance any further the United States made it known that they wanted Hamas to be left alone to form its government. We were told that the US was against any 'blurring of the line dividing Hamas from those Palestinian political forces committed to the two-state solution. Abu Mazen soon made clear that Fateh members would not participate in a Hamas-led government. The US reportedly also sent unequivocal signals to independents who had been approached about joining the government that they would be ill-advised to do so. In the event, Hamas formed a government that included some independents but was largely dominated by Hamas. This naturally facilitated the continued quarantine of the Palestinian Authority government, a.k.a. the 'Hamas Government'.

Before going on, I want to stress that, in effect, a National Unity Government with a compromise platform along the lines of Mecca might have been achieved soon after the election, in February or March 2006, had the United States not led the Quartet to set impossible demands, and opposed a National Unity Government in principle. At the time, and indeed until the Mecca Agreement a year later, the United States clearly pushed for a confrontation between Fateh and Hamas – so much so that, a week before Mecca, the US envoy declared twice in an envoys' meeting in Washington how much 'I like this violence', referring to the near-civil war that was erupting in Gaza in which civilians were being regularly killed and injured, because 'it means that other Palestinians are resisting Hamas'. Please remember this next time someone argues that the Mecca agreement, to the extent that it showed progress, proved that a year of pressure 'worked', and we should keep the isolation going. On the contrary, the same result might have been achieved much earlier without the year in between in which so much damage was done to Palestinian institutions, and so much suffering brought to the people of the occupied territory, in pursuit of a policy that didn't work, which many of us believed from the outset wouldn't work, and which, I have no doubt, is at best extremely short-sighted ...

PRESIDENT CARTER – 'ABOMINABLE' BLAIR

On 19 May, James Naughtie interviewed former US President Jimmy Carter on Radio 4's Today programme. These excerpts are taken from the interview.

BBC: How do you judge these days Mr Blair's support for Mr Bush?

Carter: Abominable. Loyal. Blind. Apparently subservient. And I think that the almost undeviating support by Great Britain for the ill-advised policies of President Bush in Iraq have been a major tragedy for the world.

BBC: This is an interesting question because the implication behind what you say is that if Mr Blair at some point, say in the year in the run up to war, had taken a step back, had moved away from Mr Bush, it would've made an important difference inside the United States. Is that what you believe?

Carter: I believe so. I can't say it would have made the definitive difference. But it would certainly have assuaged the problems that have arose lately. And so one of the defences of the Bush administration, in the American public and on a worldwide basis (it hasn't been successful in my opinion) has been that we must be more correct in our actions than the world thinks because Great Britain is backing us. And so I think the combination of Bush and Blair giving their support to this tragedy in Iraq has strengthened the effort and has made opposition less effective and has prolonged the war and increased the tragedy that has resulted.

BBC: You sound quite sad as you say that.

Carter: Yes I am sad about it because the war was unjustified, unnecessary and has wrought a tragedy on the Iraqi people, on the American people, on some of the British people, and has caused deep chasms on a global basis.

BBC: How important is it that the new Prime Minister, and we'll have one by the end of next month in this country as you know, whose support of the war, who always supported it, who paid for it as Chancellor of the Exchequer, changes policy. Is that what you hope will happen?

Carter: I would hope that that combination of less enthusiasm from Great Britain would be a factor and the rising animosity toward the war within the American public and within the United States Congress — those factors together, I hope, will expedite the exodus of the occupying forces primarily of the United States and Great Britain.

BBC: One of the interesting things that's happened in your country, as you know, in the last quarter of a century is that a kind of religious fervour has entered into politics. Now, some people probably forget that when you came into politics as President in the mid-seventies you were a man of conviction and of faith from the south and that was controversial in its time. And yet you now find yourself arguing against those who say that faith is essential to politics. It's an odd position for you to be in, isn't it?

Carter: No I don't think so. It was clear that I was a religious person, still am. But I was very meticulous in completely separating my religious faith from any element of politics of governance in the White House. I believed in what Thomas Jefferson, one of our founding fathers, said that we should build a wall between church and state and I adhere to that premise.

BBC: It's a wall that has been chipped away at in your country, hasn't it?

Carter: It has been in the last six years in particular. Yes.

BBC: Do you want to see that change?

Carter: Yes, I do and I hope it will be. I believe it will be. The current trends and public opinion polls and the results of the election last year, I think, have shown that the political influence of the fundamentalist religious believers on the one side in the White House and in Congress is dissipating.

BBC: I think you once said that you worshipped a Prince of Peace not a Prince of something else.

Carter: Not a Prince of Pre-emptive war. Yes.

BBC: Look back finally, President Carter, over the last 30 years, during which you have been performing functions from the very highest in your country, to that of an ex-president wielding all the influence that you can. Are you still an optimist, or are you sad that we are where we are?

Carter: No, I am still an optimist. I think in most ways we've reached the death of international approbation of friendship toward our country. I think the only change that is going to be likely in the future is to improve that situation. The situation in the Middle East couldn't get much worse unless an all out war erupts. I believe that future changes will be beneficial and I think that it is inevitable that within the next few months, or certainly less than a few years, we'll see an exodus of the occupying forces from Iraq. So these kinds of things I believe are almost inevitably going to improve the global situation that we now suffer.

So, I am optimistic about that. And I don't give up hope on the premise that the Middle East peace process is still viable, and if we can capitalise on future opportunities, I believe that we can have success.

NATO – A SOBER EVALUATION

Johan Galtung, founder of TRANSCEND, the peace and development network, protested about the meeting of Nato foreign ministers in Oslo on 25 April 2007. This is what he said.

Foreign Ministers of the North Atlantic Treaty Organization!

You are not welcome. The best thing about your meeting is the short duration. We wish you good riddance.

As a matter of fact, we wish you did not exist. We wish you had had the decency to dissolve like the Warsaw Treaty Organization after the Cold War.

The old Nato had a rationale, to contain Soviet aggression. About that we can discuss, but it is history.

The new Nato is offensive, not defensive. The theatre is no longer the North Atlantic arena, but the whole world. It is engaged in preventive war, rather than containing aggression, in expanding the space under Nato control, rather than in solving conflicts. In doing so, Nato creates the situations it is supposed to eliminate.

Today it looks like a major purpose is to keep Nato alive for its own sake, as a dinosaur heading for extinction. It is a tragedy to hear people claim that Nato must succeed instead of asking what is good for the Afghan people. And it is even more tragic to watch countries compensating for unwillingness to support Nato's Master, the United States of America, in Iraq by turning to Afghanistan, sacrificing Afghan lives on the altar of submission to Washington.

'North Atlantic'. That smells Anglo-America — with a dash of Norway, where you are right now located. And with a trail of blood from Palestine to Iraq to Iran to Afghanistan. Yes, it also stands for democracy and human rights. Like apartheid for the Palestinians, torture and rendition to several of you, walls of concrete and steel, repression and killing.

Democracy? Some democracy: the USA executive is not accountable
– *to the people*, but to money fuelling fake elections as in Florida and Ohio, and to the American Israel Public Affairs Committee (AIPAC) and the National Rifle Association (NRA);
– *to the judiciary*, appointed by the executive itself;
– *to the Congress*, because the President can veto any bill and the two-party system makes it very difficult to override a veto.

Is this really a model for which you are killing people, or are you simply afraid of Washington? Of being rejected by the Master, of one day being exposed to its carpets of bombs? And what does that say about the nature of Nato?

As specialists on Afghanistan, you of course know the histories of the English invasions of 1838–42 and 1878–81, which ended with a massacre of the English Embassy in Kabul, and the Soviet invasion of 1979–86, with final withdrawal in 1989. You might draw a conclusion for good or for bad: these are proud people, who want to be masters in their own land.

You have no military chance whatsoever. You cling to the idea of something

finite – 'Taliban' – that you can crush or contain. But the more you kill, the more resistance you create. And that resistance has:
– *no limit in time*. There may be lulls, but never any capitulations;
– *no limit in space*. They have the whole Muslim *UMMA*, 1.3 billion, mainly separated by borders drawn by the West, to draw upon.

And yet there are solutions in Afghanistan, for them, not you, to bring about:
– A coalition government with, not without, Talibans, negotiating, not crushing them;
– Priority to the basic needs for food, shelter, clothing, health and education for all;
– Afghanistan as a federation, not the unitary state run for foreign benefit from Kabul;
– A Central Asian Community with neighbouring nations deeply intertwined with Afghanistan;
– Security provided by the Christian-dominated UN Security Council with the Muslim Organization of the Islamic Conference.

And there are solutions to the conflict with Iran. Why are the US/UK so much more worried about a nuclear Iran and missiles flying than about a nuclear Pakistan and India? Because they think Iran hates them. And why should Iran hate them? In one word: 1953. The CIA – MI6 coup against a legally elected Prime Minister, Mossadegh, installing the Shah and 25 years of dictatorship. And how does one handle that? By a one-minute Bush/Blair speech accepting responsibility and apologizing. Do you Foreign Ministers have the courage to tell the self-righteous Anglo-Americans to do so?

And there are solutions to Iraq, not any stupid 'reconciliation' without political solutions, better known as pacification. US/UK and the remaining coalition partners stop killing, shed their uniforms, apologize, compensate, clean up, and ask the UN to convene a Conference on Security and Cooperation in West Asia, like the Helsinki Conference 1973-75 model. The fate of Iraq — possibly as a community more than as a state – is for the Iraqis to decide.

And there are solutions to what your Master calls terrorism – in your midst you have a country called Spain, whose leader, Zapatero, did after 11 March 2004 what Bush and Blair should have done after 9/11 and 07/07. He stopped killing Arab Muslims in Iraq. He legalized migrants from Morocco. He started negotiating with Morocco instead of bombing. And he organized a Dialogue of Civilizations. Use Spain rather than US/UK as the model.

But you have a huge problem: your Master. With more than 70 interventions on its conscience after the Second World War, with somewhere between 13 and 17 million killed in overt actions. You are allies. With few exceptions, you are silent. Silence means consent – to one of the worst crimes in history: US/UK in Iraq.

There is one way out. You stand up against your Master rather than mimicking the Master's Voice with some corridor whispering.

You can walk out.
You can say stop.
You can say: enough killing!
Let us solve all these conflicts, and let us turn the adversaries of our Master's creation into our friends.

Reviews

What Price the Planet?

Al Gore, *An Inconvenient Truth*, Bloomsbury, 2006, 324 pages, ISBN 978-0747589068, £14.99
Steve Jones, *Coral: A Pessimist in Paradise*, Little Brown, 2007, 242 pages, ISBN 978-0316729383, £15.99
Larry Lohman, *Carbon Dating* in *Development Dialogue*, no. 48, September 2006, 360 pages, Hammarskjold Foundation, Sweden
Colin Leys & Leo Panich, *Coming to Terms with Nature*, Socialist Register, 2007, 364 pages, Merlin Press, ISBN 978-0850365788, £14.95
James Lovelock, *The Revenge of Gaia*, Penguin, Allen Lane, 2006, 192 pages, ISBN 978-0713999143, £16.99

It has been said that human beings are the only animals which foul their own nest. The damage we have done to our planet, Earth, is detailed in these books, with due warnings of the destruction that is to come if we do not change our ways. The main threat comes from our insatiable extraction of fossil carbon deposits from the earth's surface to fuel our whole economic system, and the release of these deposits as carbon dioxide into the air and oceans with the consequent global warming. At the same time we are cutting down forests, over-fishing the seas, ruining the coral reefs, polluting the air, turning land into desert, while expanding populations as if the resources of the planet were endless. These are the matters dealt with in these books, but all the authors who, with the exception of Al Gore, are scientific experts in their own fields, regard global warming as the most serious threat, and all see this as primarily the result of human actions. Sun spots and the wobble of the earth on its axis are not regarded as the prime suspects. And yet, one cannot forget that it was only 70,000 years ago that the last ice age ended, and the coming and going of this massive climate change was sudden and no fault of the tiny human population on earth at the time.

The main concern of all these authors is naturally, what can be done in time to avert total human catastrophe. In the much vaunted Kyoto Protocol the governments of the Developed Countries, the main perpetrators of carbon emission, promised to make planned reductions in their emissions. President Bush withdrew the United States from this agreement, since he did not believe in global warming, but the US negotiators had already inserted into the Kyoto Protocol a whole series of measures for a system of carbon trading which would allow the big energy companies to buy exemptions from the planned carbon reductions. These have not been so widely advertised, but they form the substance of the 350 page Swedish study under review and of one of the *Socialist Register* studies. In effect these exemptions make a nonsense of the whole agreement. As one wit put it, it is as if a bigamist or polygamist found an unmarried person or persons of the same sex who were then paid to abstain from marriage so that their illegal practices could continue. It is in fact worse than this. First, because it is the poor countries which are persuaded to contribute to the rich countries' immunities. Second, because there is no adequate regulation of the bargains, many of which are phoney, and the result is that no actual cuts in carbon emissions are made. The allocation of carbon allowances, so-called 'emission rights' under the Kyoto Protocol, was made to countries at a certain percentage below what they said they were emitting in 1990. Then these rights in Europe were transferred to countries which transferred them to their several industrial sectors, leading in the case of the United Kingdom to annual 'gifts' in excess of actual average emissions over the years 1998-2003 (*Carbon Trading* Table 2. p.89).

When it comes to the *trading* of rights by individual companies, this has been compared to the medieval Christian practice of the sale of indulgencies to offset sins (Achim Brunnengraber of the Free University of Berlin in *Socialist Register*, p.220). Two instruments are provided to states – to issue certificates corresponding to their assigned amount of emissions. Trading is planned for 2008 onwards. One instrument, the Joint Implementation provision (JI), relates to projects involving investment in carbon reducing measures in an industrial country (mostly Eastern Europe) by another such country. The other, the Clean Development Mechanism (CDM), relates to investment in a Developing Country. Several hundred projects were already under consideration by June 2006. Examples of such investments are more efficient power stations, windmills and water power and, most popular, forestation schemes. These investments can then be set as credits against reduction obligations. There are several difficulties about both Joint Implementations and Clean Development Mechanisms. Such investments might have taken place without this incentive and it is not easy to calculate what the actual carbon savings are and how comparable they are to what is being reduced from the investor's carbon emission obligations.

The Swedish study of *Carbon Trading* emphasises an even more serious objection. The United States experience of controlling pollution through marketing devices, on which the Kyoto measures were based, has revealed that in the words of the Heinrich Böll Foundation of Berlin 'the "polluter pays" principle has been turned into "the polluter buys his way out principle".' The result is that emissions markets are only stop-gap measures, structurally biased against the kind of radical change needed to tackle global warming. (*Carbon Trading*, p.117).They do nothing to end the way the capitalist economy is 'locked in', often by state subsidies and by the International Financial Institutions' programmes, to high fossil fuel use – in military spending, untaxed airplane fuel, motorways, out of town supermarkets, centralised power plants, etc. Similarly, the emphasis on trading and markets brings in the whole panoply of financial mediation – jobbers and brokers, consultants and lawyers, insurance and speculation – the very heart of the capitalist system.

The *Socialist Register's* issue on 'Coming to Terms with Nature' is aimed to find a socialist alternative to the dictates of capital. The unsustainable nature of the capitalist system is explored in several essays and the implications of disaster made clear, but answers are not evident. The trading answer is well disposed of, but nothing put in its place except suggestions of 'far-reaching structural change'. The volume ends with a lament at the failure of 'red' and 'green' forces to work together. The contribution by Frieder Otto Wolf, one-time German Euro-MP, offers a particularly tragic account of the failure of the German Greens to build an eco-socialist national party. A final contribution recognises, however, the limits to 'eco-localism'. The *Socialist Register* editors in the end hope only that the essays will provoke discussion and perhaps rescue the possibility of democratic planning from the 'failed practices of authoritarian communism'.

Al Gore's book, which is beautifully illustrated (but rather irritatingly studded with pictures of him and his family) and now made into a film, describes in detail just what is happening to the planet as a result of global warming, and what will happen if no steps are taken to reduce carbon use, but it has a rather limited list of recommendations. Apart from carbon trading and especially tree planting, he pleads for a more responsible consumerism among individual families. It is hardly the 'catalyst for change' which he hopes for.

Steve Jones, Professor of Genetics at University College London, gave the Reith lectures in 1991 and is the author of several books of popular science. His book *Coral: A Pessimist in Paradise* I have included in this review because of the beauty of his writing, fitting the beauty of its subject, which our pollution of the seas has almost destroyed, but he has no expectation that human folly will cease. The coral reefs, he concludes, 'only remind us that our extinction is as certain as is theirs. Whether it will take place in the slow course of evolutionary time or in the near future, as our own imprudence causes Nature to take her revenge, neither Newton nor Darwin can tell.'

No review of books on the prospects for the planet earth would be complete without mention of James Lovelock's concept of 'Gaia', the Greek earth goddess who gave her name to all the words we have which begin with 'ge'. 'Gaia' for Lovelock is a biosphere which has evolved as an 'active adaptive control system able to maintain the earth in homeostasis' – an equilibrium temperature for organisms' growth and optimum acidity, salinity and oxygen. It is all this which human greed and imprudence are destroying with inevitable dire consequences for the future of the planet and life on it.

Lovelock is a distinguished English scientist, Companion of Honour, author of over 200 scientific papers and three books, who at the age of 86 has written this warning book on 'Why the earth is fighting back and how we can save humanity'. The warnings are spelt out with full scientific evidence, carefully cited mainly from the Inter-governmental Panel on Climate Change (IPCC). While global warming is accepted as a natural phenomenon between ice ages, human activity from our excessive consumption of energy using up the carbon deposits in the earth's surface is enormously speeding up the process so as to melt down the ice caps, raising sea levels to a height which will flood many of the world's major cities. On top of this we have been polluting the oceans and destroying the earth's forest cover both of which absorbed much of the carbon dioxide (CO_2) released by the consumption practices of our rapidly increasing population.

Lovelock does not believe that any of the measures being proposed to halt the warming process – by converting from coal, oil and gas to hydro, wind power, solar, hydrogen and biofuels or by tree planting , let alone carbon trading – will work in time to prevent disaster. There is no such thing, he believes, as sustainable development, only sustainable retreat. We have to learn to replace economic growth by economic reduction, but how within the next 30 years? Lovelock sees the only hope in bringing up our children to have faith in a Gaia who expects care and restraint rather than in a God who requires them to be 'fruitful and multiply and replenish the earth and subdue it'. In the meantime, he says that 'we should now be preparing for a rise of sea level, spells of near intolerable heat like that in Central Europe in 2003 and storms of unprecedented severity'. 'The immediate need', he goes on, 'is safe and secure sources of energy to keep the lights of civilisation burning and for the preparation of our defences against rising sea levels'. And here he will offend most conservationists by recommending nuclear fission, until our scientists can master nuclear fusion.

Michael Barratt Brown

Attlee's Life

Francis Beckett, *Clem Attlee***, Politico's, 2007, 338 pages, paperback ISBN 9781842751923, £14.99**

Francis Beckett's biography of Clem Attlee was first published in 1997. This new edition is very much to be welcomed. It includes a few revisions made as a result of subsequent interviews conducted by the author. They add to the understanding of Attlee's role in the evolution of Labour's policy during his period as Labour leader and as Prime Minister.

Beckett's book is well written and compels attention from the first page to the last. The material for it was well researched, covering the entire period of Attlee's association with the labour movement from the time when he first joined the Independent Labour Party in 1907 until his death some 60 years later. It is a sympathetic biography about Attlee's opinions and actions, but it gives a fair showing to the standpoint of those in the Labour Party who were to his left, notably Aneurin Bevan.

What emerges is a rounded portrait of Attlee as a man with a deep commitment to social justice, a determination to eliminate poverty, deprivation and squalor, and an inclination to the left rather than to the right of the labour movement. He was convinced of the indispensable role of the Labour Party as an instrument of social change within a parliamentary democracy. He was happy with a party structure based fundamentally upon trade union affiliations and individual membership.

Attlee was, nevertheless, influenced by the circumstances of his birth and upbringing. He was born into a well-to-do upper middle class family. His father was a prosperous solicitor who, in 1906, became the President of the Law Society. In politics his father supported the more radical wing of the Liberal Party. Clement Attlee's childhood was spent in a very comfortable home with the amenities of the time and servants to meet the domestic needs of the family.

Clement Attlee had the education expected by his social origin: attendance at a fashionable public school, Haileybury, followed by admission to and graduation from Oxford University. He became a lawyer, though he had little enthusiasm for legal work.

In 1906 he was introduced to a boys' club in a slum area in Limehouse in the East End of London. It was known as Haileybury House, and had been established by some former pupils of the Haileybury public school to help clergy, who were also Old Haileyburians, and who were active in the area. This introduction to the poverty and deprivation of the East End was to transform Clement Attlee's life and thinking. By 1907 he was working and living in the area. From being a young man with not very strong views he became a socialist and joined the ILP. At that time, the Stepney branch of the ILP had about 20 members.

Attlee had his initiation as a very nervous political speaker at a small open-air meeting in a street in Stepney. His audience consisted of a few ILP members and a very small number of passers-by. Shortly afterwards he stood as an ILP candidate for the Stepney Borough Council. He polled 67 votes. By this time, politics was beginning to dominate his life.

When the First World War began in 1914 Attlee volunteered for service almost immediately. Many active ILP members opposed the war and became conscientious objectors. Attlee's elder brother was a conscientious objector. Attlee's reasons for enlisting were very unusual. He later wrote that he did not accept the cry of 'Your King and Country Need You', nor was he 'convinced of Germany's sole guilt'. On the other hand, he said that it appeared wrong to him to let others make a sacrifice whilst he stood by, especially as he was unmarried. He fought in the army at Gallipoli, was wounded fighting near Suez, and was finally posted to the Western Front in Europe. He was promoted to the rank of Major.

After his demobilisation Clement Attlee returned to Stepney and renewed his activity in the labour movement. In November 1919 Labour won a majority in the municipal elections in Stepney, and Attlee was appointed Mayor of the borough. Shortly afterwards he became the chairman of the Association of Labour Mayors in London boroughs. In 1922 he was elected to Parliament for the Stepney constituency of Limehouse. He was re-elected in 1924 and became a junior Minister in the first ever Labour government. He was again elected in 1929 with a substantial majority, and in 1930 was appointed to the government as the Chancellor of the Duchy of Lancaster. In the following year he became Postmaster General.

In the crisis of 1931, which led to the downfall of the Labour Government, Clem Attlee sided with those who refused to accept cuts in unemployment benefit. He supported the expressed opposition of the trade union movement. The Labour Prime Minister and Chancellor of the Exchequer, together with a number of other

MPs, broke away and joined with the Conservatives and a number of Liberals to form a National Government. It secured a huge majority of more than 500 in the succeeding General Election. Labour was reduced to 46 MPs, of whom only three had Front Bench experience: George Lansbury, Stafford Cripps and Clement Attlee.

George Lansbury was elected as Leader of the Parliamentary Party and Attlee as Deputy Leader. Attlee admired Lansbury and loyally served under him. In 1935 Lansbury resigned after being attacked by Ernest Bevin at the Labour Party conference because of his pacifist response to Italy's attack on Abyssinia. The conference called for sanctions against Italy. This was not supported by either Lansbury or Cripps, but was supported by Attlee.

The 1935 General Election was lost by Labour, though the party increased its representation to 154 MPs. A new leader had to be elected. On the first ballot there were three candidates: Attlee, Herbert Morrison and Arthur Greenwood. Attlee secured the most votes on the first ballot but did not have an absolute majority. Arthur Greenwood was eliminated. On the second ballot Attlee defeated Morrison by 88 votes to 48.

Thus began the final ascent to the future return of a majority Labour Government with Attlee as leader. In 1945 he became Prime Minister after a General Election in which Labour secured an overall majority of 146. It was a memorable and sensational victory. The Conservatives were led by Winston Churchill. Labour's election manifesto called for economic planning, the extension of social ownership, a radical programme of social welfare and the building of affordable houses.

What is the evidence to justify the view – or to contradict the view – that Attlee preferred to lead from the left of centre rather than from the right of centre of the labour movement? There can be no doubt of his very strong views about social security. He became Prime Minister at a time of great economic difficulty at the end of the Second World War, but he was totally committed to bringing about improvements in social welfare. He carried out Labour's programme.

The National Insurance Act, the Industrial Injuries Act, the National Assistance Act, the housing programme and, above all, the introduction of the National Health Service, justified the claim that, in comparison with anything that had existed before, Labour was in the process of establishing a 'welfare state'. This could not have been done without the dedication of the Prime Minister. Moreover, he appointed and supported Aneurin Bevan, the principal figure on the left of the Party, to lead the thrust on health and housing.

One of the principal figures on the right of the Parliamentary Party, and perhaps the principal figure, was Herbert Morrison. It was more than a difference of personality that led Attlee to be wary of him. There were differences of political approach. One of the earliest differences centred on the imprisonment of George Lansbury, the then leader of Poplar Council, who, following the First World War, joined with other Labour councillors in refusing to pay the borough's precepts to the London County Council, then under Conservative control. The Poplar councillors wanted to use the money to help the unemployed. Attlee supported Lansbury. Morrison, the leader of the neighbouring Hackney Council, denounced Lansbury.

In the second half of the 1930s, Attlee was firm in his support for the Popular Front Government of Spain in its resistance to the revolt of General Franco and the armed assistance given to Franco by the fascist dictators of Italy and Germany. Attlee denounced the British Government for its one-sided policy of so called non-intervention, which made it 'an accessory to the attempt to murder democracy in Spain'.

Up to the year 1936 the constituency representatives on the National Executive Committee of the Labour Party were elected by the whole of the annual conference. This meant, in effect, that the big unions had the predominant influence. Attlee was among those who pressed that the constituencies should elect their own representatives on the NEC. In 1937 this right was granted. For years afterwards – indeed to the present time – this change has ensured the presence of left-wingers on the NEC.

Attlee played a key role in the decision of the 1945 Labour Government to recognise the right of Indian independence. Power was transferred without political or military resistance from Britain. It was an historic step forward.

Attlee's influence was also important, indeed decisive, in preventing the expulsion of Aneurin Bevan from the Labour Party in 1954 after Bevan had led 62 Labour MPs in opposition to the Government's support for nuclear weapons. Arthur Deakin, the then leader of the TGWU, was frustrated in his attempt to exclude Aneurin Bevan.

After these many indications of the left-of-centre influence of Attlee, how was it then, it might be asked, that the Labour Government under the leadership of Attlee committed itself to US leadership in the initial stages of the Cold War? The consequences of this decision – a heavy rearmament programme, a stringent wages policy at a time of rising profits and prices, the introduction of a two-year period of conscription to the armed forces, charges for certain NHS services, brakes on the housing programme and support for German rearmament – led eventually to a strong movement of dissent within the labour movement. It culminated in the resignation of Aneurin Bevan, Harold Wilson and John Freeman from the Labour Government.

The answer to this question is that in 1945 Attlee did not begin his premiership with the intention of being a partisan in a Cold War. Francis Beckett provides evidence in his book that at the beginning of the Cold War Attlee was less responsive to US pressure than the Foreign Secretary, Ernest Bevin. He changed in 1947. He was undoubtedly influenced by Ernest Bevin, whom he admired. Bevin had stood by the Labour Party in 1931-32, and his example influenced the trade union movement. Francis Beckett suggests that from that period Attlee and Bevin were 'soulmates'.

Secondly, Attlee was certainly influenced by Britain's very difficult economic situation in the post-war period. The economic pressure of the US Government under Truman, and the possible dire consequences for the British economy if the British Government failed to support the US in the 'Cold War' were, no doubt, very much in his mind.

Thirdly, by 1947 it was becoming clear that within Eastern Europe the Soviet Union was determined to consolidate its grip, even to the point of purging communist leaders who did not 'toe the line' on every issue. Other political leaders who were not communists had little or no opportunity for democratic dissent.

For those of us who remain proud of so many of the achievements of the 1945 Labour Government and of the role of Attlee, it is necessary to acknowledge that in the controversies symbolised by the Bevanite movement of dissent, 'Keep Left', it was the dissenters who were right in warning of the dangers of the alignment of Britain with many aspects of US foreign policy.

It is worth adding an important footnote in relation to the attitude of Attlee. According to evidence available to Francis Beckett, Attlee would have preferred Aneurin Bevan to Hugh Gaitskell as Leader of the Party, though he believed it was not possible at the time for Bevan to secure the leadership. Francis Beckett also reveals that Attlee preferred Harold Wilson to Hugh Gaitskell.

J.E.Mortimer

Bukharin's Prison Writings

Nikolai Bukharin, translated by George Shriver, *Socialism and Its Culture*, 258 pages, Seagull Books, ISBN 978 1 90542 222 7, £16.99

Up-to-the-minute capitalist globalism here presents itself at the service of ancient Communism. The Prison Manuscripts of Nikolai Bukharin, written in unbelievable 'medieval' circumstances during his detention prior to the mock trial which sentenced him to death, have been appearing in a series of volumes from different publishers. I reviewed one of these a year ago, but here there appears another, typeset in Calcutta and printed in Kings Lynn. This example of international capitalist co-operation stands in marked contrast (which would have astonished Bukharin) to the troubled evolution of the former Soviet Union. Where, today, is the

> 'respect and comradeship in the relations between collective farmers of Turkmenistan and those of Ukraine, those of Tajikistan and those of Georgia, those of the Moscow region and those of Azerbaijan, those of Siberia, and those of Birobijan (the Jewish autonomous region in the Soviet Far East) ...'?

It is unfortunately hazardous to believe one's own propaganda too deeply, and this kind of belief is a hallmark of Bukharin's posthumous book. He argues that the mutual respect and comradeship of the farmers

> 'is evident at the congresses held by collective farmers where the most important decisions are made in common.'

It is true that some collective farms have survived in a relatively healthy condition, especially in Belarus. But the collegiality of decision making withered long since, if it had ever truly existed.

Of course, Bukharin was locked in prison, with no access to research materials, and he had to write from memory. Equally significantly, he was actually writing for a known audience of one, who alone held the power of life and death over him. This was not a time to try to induct Stalin into a more objective understanding of social conditions in the Soviet Union, and of the relative powers of different social groups there. Whatever Bukharin said would have to echo official propaganda in all substantial matters. The only relative freedom of movement would be in matters of high ideology.

Even here, flatulent slogans are by no means avoided.

> 'The USSR is showing the world a model of brotherhood and unity among nationalities. This is not the abstract cosmopolitanism of a utopian rationalist who fails to see the real particularities and distinctive features among nationalities ...'

There would soon be time to explore these real particularities when whole nationalities were being deported, very shortly after Bukharin's own extinction. This trauma had effects which lived on long after the Second World War, and erupted in a series of bloody conflicts in the declining years of the USSR, which persist and indeed get worse.

In short, Bukharin's parting thoughts have not weathered well. Since they were marshalled under such adverse conditions, it is not really reasonable to expect that they might. Quite aside from any appeal for clemency for himself, which must have been a part of his thinking, even if unstated, these prison writings were certainly aimed at securing a reprieve for his wife and young son, Anna Larina and Yuri. Anna was half his age, and very beautiful. He doted on her. But in fact, Anna had already been sent to the Gulag before these writings were finished, and Yuri was already placed into foster care.

Steve Cohen, Bukharin's biographer, who describes his valiant efforts to recover the Prison Manuscripts, tells us how Anna and Yuri were reunited, after she had made a prolonged journey through Stalin's prisons, labour camps and Siberian exile, and after Yuri had spent two decades under a different family name, in various foster homes and orphanages. Brought together again in 1956, they met up with Bukharin's biographer before the rehabilitation in 1988.

Bukharin was a cultivated man and could be highly persuasive. But he was also capable of lucid analysis and sober political judgement, which qualities are not very evident in these Prison Manuscripts. If Stalin's purge of the old Bolsheviks was not simply an aberration, then it needed explanation. Evidently this cannot be found in these pages. Attempts to explain would certainly bring down on those who were presumptuous enough to embark upon them, condign punishment.

This was the fate of Trotsky, who was already in exile, and who was, in 1940, murdered by a KGB agent in Mexico (as is now known, with direct support from Moscow). It happens that Trotsky had published, in 1936, his remarkable book on

The Revolution Betrayed. Readers of Bukharin's Prison Manuscripts will be mainly motivated by the desire to understand the poignant tragedy of their author. If they are looking for a real light on the subject of the manuscripts, then they should certainly begin their reading with *The Revolution Betrayed*, however far they may subsequently succeed in going beyond it.

Since 1936 we in the West have also become familiar with another Russian voice, which was not at that time very widely available. This was the voice of André Platonov, a certified 'unstable element' who left the Communist Party in 1921. It was only a year after Bukharin's rehabilitation that saw the publication in the Soviet Union of *The Foundation Pit*, which had been written long before, from 1929-30. A group of workers are digging an immense pit, to lay the foundations of a colossal building, intended to house the local proletariat in its entirety. This, of course, is destined never to be built.

Platonov captures the extraordinary mixture of hope and despair 'by which many ordinary people must have lived during Stalin's revolution from above'. Perhaps those who seek to understand Bukharin's tortured last manuscripts, to do him justice need Platonov as their guide.

Ken Coates

Africa Education

Michael Wolfers, *Thomas Hodgkin: Wandering Scholar*, Merlin Press, 2007, 256 pages, hardback ISBN 9780850365801, £40, paperback ISBN 9780850365818, £16.95

Thomas Hodgkin (1910-1982) was a crusader for the education and advancement of the peoples of Africa and of the developing countries in general and a pioneer in the study of the pre-colonial history of sub-Saharan Africa. In 2000, Thomas' daughter, Elizabeth, and Michael Wolfers published his *Letters from Africa 1947-56*, sent mainly to his wife, Dorothy Crowfoot Hodgkin, O.M., a Nobel chemistry laureate. These represent a fascinating and informed commentary on Africa during the period of the transition from colonialism to independence. Michael Wolfers has now followed this up with a detailed biography of the author of these letters, which provides a gripping account of a life devoted to learning and the cause of human emancipation.

Thomas Hodgkin was a scion of an affluent, intellectual and well-connected family whose roots go back to seventeenth century Cotswold Quakers. His paternal grandfather, Thomas Hodgkin, was a banker and historian, who wrote *Italy and Her Invaders* in eight volumes: his maternal grandfather, A. L. Smith, was a pioneer of the Workers' Educational Association and Master of Balliol College, Oxford; his father, Robin Hodgkin, was Provost of Queen's College, Oxford and a historian, who wrote *A History of the Anglo-Saxons* in two volumes. Family relationships and friendships linked him to establishment figures from

Archbishop William Temple to well-known poets, archaeologists, academics, civil servants and politicians.

After completing his education at Winchester and Balliol, Thomas was appointed to the Palestine Civil Service in 1934, at the time of the British mandate. Having already developed left-wing views, he became increasingly uncomfortable about British repression of the Arabs for opposing unlimited Jewish immigration and resigned his position. Back in London, he joined the Communist Party, participated in demonstrations and wrote for the League Against Imperialism and *Labour Monthly*. He tried secondary school teaching, but decided it was not for him and moved into WEA lecturing – eventually securing a post as a WEA tutor in North Staffordshire in 1939. This brought him into contact with George Wigg, a former regular soldier, who was the North Staffs WEA district secretary.

Thomas' post was regarded as a reserved occupation and he continued in it throughout the Second World War. He helped George Wigg to lobby for Army education and, in the 1945 General Election, took part in the campaign in which Wigg was elected as the Labour MP for Dudley. In return, George Wigg pushed him to apply for the secretaryship of the University of Oxford Delegacy for Extra-Mural Studies, and to promote the university extension course in Africa when he was appointed.

This led to a succession of extended trips to Africa, during the course of which he became familiar with nationalist and religious leaders, businessmen, trade unionists, writers, journalists and others, in addition to initiating higher education on a significant scale. When the Cold War led to anti-Communist witch-hunting, Thomas resigned from the Communist Party in 1949 and from the Oxford Extra-Mural Delegacy in 1952.

He was, however, sufficiently well known as an expert on Africa to support himself by lecturing and writing. In 1956, he produced a widely acclaimed book, *Nationalism in Colonial Africa*. Along with Basil Davidson, he helped lead the way in encouraging the study of African history. His *Nigerian Perspectives*, first published in 1960, with an enlarged second edition in 1975, became a seminal source for historians of Africa. In addition, he wrote innumerable articles and contributed to other books. In 1981, he published *Vietnam: The Revolutionary Path*.

He regarded himself as a Marxist, but he was not dogmatic. Although he rejoined the Communist Party in 1976, after 27 years, it was never at the centre of his activity. He was, however, totally committed to progressive causes. I remember his unflagging support for Liberation's campaign against the execution, detention and ill-treatment of political prisoners by President Nimeiry of the Sudan in the early 1970s.

Michael Wolfers' book is a magnificent record of a fascinating life. In addition to its political content, it provides much information on Thomas' personal idiosyncrasies, his permissive attitudes, his relationships with people in all walks of life, and his extended and talented family. I had difficulty in putting it down before I had finished reading it.

All who are interested in Africa and the developing countries, in historical research and in learning more about this outstanding personality should read this book. I recommend it without reservation.

Stan Newens
with grateful acknowledgements to Liberation

Fire over Fylingdales

Blaise Vyner, *Fylingdales – Wildfire and Archaeology*, North York Moors National Park, 2007, 44 pages, ISBN 978 1 904622 14 3, £5.75

The journey by road from York to Whitby, on the north-east coast of England, takes you over the empty uplands of the North York Moors. At the town of Pickering, a red sign points north towards 'RAF Fylingdales'. Then the road climbs steadily, running beside the great declivity known as The Hole of Horcum, before pitching sharply downwards. There, up on the right, stands a three-sided, truncated, concrete pyramid at the centre of 'RAF Fylingdales'.

Fylingdales provides a major link in the chain that makes up the United States' Ballistic Missile Early Warning System that encircles the northern hemisphere. Other stations in the system are at Thule in Greenland and Clear in Alaska. Fylingdales sends data directly to US Space Command in Cheyenne Mountain, Colorado Springs. It also forms part of a growing network comprising the globally dispersed anti-ballistic missile system which the US is developing apace, following President Bush's unilateral withdrawal, in 2002, from the Anti-Ballistic Missile Treaty which his country had concluded with the Soviet Union thirty years earlier.

In September 2003, the North Yorkshire base was almost engulfed. A wildfire swept across Fylingdales Moor, burning everything in its path. Amidst the ashes of the vegetation was revealed a variety of ancient features. These included examples of 'rock art' – rocks decorated with cup-marks and other motifs – some of them dating from the late Neolithic period, 5,000 years ago.

'The wildfire presented both an opportunity and a challenge,' according to Blaise Vyner, the author of this short account published by the North York Moors National Park. 'The opportunity was to record the detail of the archaeology: the challenge was to do this before the urgent regeneration of the vegetation.' Now, according to the author, the overall detail of the archaeology of Fylingdales Moor is better known than anywhere else on the North York Moors. Before the fire there were some 150 known archaeological sites; now there are more than 2,000.

The fire left a blackened moonscape. This is graphically represented in an exhibition at Whitby Museum called 'Fire Over Fylingdales', for which project this short guide has been produced. Blackened wood from the Moor forms naturalistic sculptures. In amongst the photographs of stranded leverets and displaced hawks there is one of the 120 foot high pyramid, which houses a solid-state phased-array radar (SSPAR) with a range of 3,000 miles. Above it flies a Spitfire aircraft, commemorating earlier campaigns. The background is suffused with orange. The wildfire came very close to the base.

Whose ballistic missiles might Fylingdales give early warning of? In 2002, members of Subterranea Britannica, 'a society devoted to the study and investigation of man-made ... and man-used underground places', toured the site. An informative account of their visit posted online (www.subbrit.org.uk) records that:

> 'Our hosts ran a tape of a missile launch from the Barents Sea which had been recorded some time earlier and we were able to see the plot appear on screen and follow the drill and identification of the object to validation point. We all asked heaps of questions and were told that there had not been a validated launch call for at least three years although one was made some time ago when a Soviet Typhoon class submarine launched a test missile from the polar ice cap towards Russia. Normally all sides involved in test launches of ballistic missiles notifies (sic) everyone else so as not to cause false alarms of attack. On this occasion the Russians hadn't informed anybody and tensions were said to have been "high".'

More tense moments at RAF Fylingdales look likely as the US pushes ahead with plans to extend its missile defence network by upgrading the facility at Fylingdales itself, while constructing a completely new radar in the Czech Republic and installing interceptor missiles in Poland. The Pentagon has also expressed a wish to place a radar base in the Caucasus. In response, the Russians are testing new long-range ballistic missiles which they say can beat the interceptors.

During the long history of human habitation on Fylingdales Moor, the fortress erected around RAF Fylingdales surely marks a low point.

Tony Simpson

Why do we still have a Bank of England?

Andrew McDonald (editor), *Reinventing Britain: Constitutional Change under New Labour,* **Politico's Publishing, 2007, 288 pages, hardback ISBN 978-1842752081, £19.99**

Reinventing Britain is the timely publication of a series of essays investigating constitutional change under New Labour. No sooner is this handy review of the range of constitutional changes brought in under the Blair administration published than the incoming Prime Minister, Gordon Brown, publishes a green paper entitled 'The Governance of Britain', promising a debate on the possibility of a written British constitution and Bill of Rights and granting Parliament the right to vote on legislation arising from international agreements such as the recently agreed European Union amending treaty.

In terms of quantity, the legislative work pursued since 1997 amounted to 41 separate pieces of legislation, not including that pertaining to Northern Ireland. Looking at this workload one is struck by the fact that it difficult to view it as a discernible programme underpinned and steered by an overriding idea of what should constitute a constitution for a 21st century nation state. Three themes do appear: the decentralisation of power through, in the case of Scotland and Wales, devolution; the rights of citizens combined with a more open society; and, almost as an add-on, the reform of the judiciary.

The lack of an overarching idea of the direction the reforms were to take taxes Lord Falconer of Thoroton QC in the foreword where he explains that 'it is egalitarianism that that has shaped our approach to constitutional reform. It is no longer acceptable that hereditary peers should dominate the House of Lords'. Fine words as long as you leave your brain in idle and pass by the thought that Lord Falconer owes his position to the pernicious system of patronage, which has been ruthlessly exploited by his former school chum and flatmate Tony Blair. In typical unabashed New Labour fashion he tells us that 'Our ambition (Old Fetesians, I presume) was to leave behind the politics of division and to nurture an egalitarian society'. What he didn't explain was that their way of doing this would be to dissolve the Labour Party as the traditional champion of the class of the politically dispossessed.

Whilst not disagreeing with the argument that society should be underpinned by a commitment to human rights, New Labour's love affair with this concept is, I'm afraid, based on the neoconservative view of individual rights which, happily for them, is designed to atomise any possibility of organising a collective response to a social wrong.

Devolution has provided us with an interesting case study. Who would have thought, even one year ago, that Scotland, Wales and Northern Ireland would be governed by executives containing nationalists. The curse of Mr Blair's sofa extended far and wide such that his cosy behind-the-scenes dealing with the devolved executives, when they were run by Labour, has brought into relief imperfections in the constitutional settlement. A recent front page in the Scottish newspaper *The Herald* illustrates the point with the headline 'Warning to Labour MPs over "wrecking the Union"'. The strong words from Jack Straw, Westminster's Justice Secretary in charge of constitutional matters, who warned his English parliamentary colleagues that they were on 'very dangerous ground', illustrate alarm that not only are David Cameron's Conservatives raising the so-called English Question early into a Brown premiership, but so also are Labour MPs south of the border. What is more, it is a devilishly difficult problem to solve. In England the problem is perceived to be the unfairness of Scottish MPs voting on purely English matters, which are now devolved. Plus there is the fact that the so-called Barnett Formula, which divides tax revenues within the United Kingdom between the devolved nations, is perceived to be unfair. In Scotland the SNP has undoubtedly attracted the radicals on which Labour has historically relied for its majorities simply because New Labour has been ignoring their demands in order to woo the voters in England, who will now be the ones most likely to be whipped up by the *Daily Mail* and *Telegraph* over what they perceive as an unfair distribution of mainly English tax revenues.

Brown's response to this 'Gordian' knot is nothing more than a smoke screen. Elements of his plan to deliver a new 'constitutional settlement' for Britain have been designed to ensure that he cannot be accused of being a Scottish prime minister influencing and controlling key parts of the English establishment, ranging from the Church of England to senior positions in England's ancient seats of learning.

One also has to question New Labour's past record on openness and reform within the Party. The Party's Policy Forums are designed to be held behind closed doors. No votes are taken, and the outcomes are invariably identical to the executive paper on which they started the discussions. The so-called Warwick agreement with the trade unions is a case in point. Agreed to get money from the unions before the 2005 election, and buried without even a decent funeral after the elections.

There is no doubt that *Reinventing Britain* is a handy reference base for locating the setting-off point for Brown's grandly titled 'The Governance of Britain', but closer examination of the latter document does not excite. For instance, on sending troops into armed conflict the reality will be that government whips will prevail. A pre-Queen's Speech debate will most likely mean the Government will still push its programme through. A written constitution will follow the logic of the British position regarding the European Union Charter of Rights with little for the labour movement to cheer about. I could go on but it is important to note that a new web site has appeared in Scotland under the banner 'Constitutional Convention'. Devolution has always been considered to be a process in Scotland, or North Britain, as Gordon Brown may soon prefer to call it. But if he is so keen on Britishness, why do we still have a Bank of England, and why are agreements with Ireland always Anglo-Irish?

Henry McCubbin

Second World War

Harry Ratner, *A Socialist at War: In the Pioneer Corps*, Socialist Platform Ltd, BCM 7646, London WC1N 3XX

Harry Ratner enlisted in the Pioneer Corps during the Second World War, and here records a most unusual memoir. He believes that the pioneers have had a bad press, and is anxious to put the record straight on this matter. But Harry was also a Trotskyist, who believed the war to be an imperialist undertaking on both sides, so that his point of view was unusual to say the least. It certainly complicated his life at the time, but he has no regrets about that, in spite of the fact that he has changed his opinions about Trotskyism, and, indeed, Marxism. From his independent standpoint, he records a strikingly objective picture, engaging in its honesty. The colonels will not want the Corps to be celebrated by so unconventional an historian, but there may be many others who can replace them as avid readers.

JP

Belltoons

Steve Bell, *My Vision for a New You*, Methuen in association with Guardian Books, 164 pages, hardback ISBN 9780413775933, £12.99

'You can be successful just like Tony Blair. Use this guide and you can reach your goals. Don't and you won't. Steve Bell dreamed up this book based on long imaginary conversations with Britain's [once] most powerful man. In his day job Steve Bell is an award winning political cartoonist for The Guardian.'

So reads the blurb for Steve Bell's eighth collection of cartoons, some of which decorate this issue. Readers of *The Spokesman* will, of course, already be very familiar with his work. We gladly celebrate this addition to the list.

TS